praise for revolutions of our times

"Every day, throughout the world, marginalized groups wage scattered struggles against their oppression, sometimes winning concessions and often losing, but it is only when poverty, repression, and constant insults to human dignity reach unbearable proportions that the people as a whole rise up against a regime. The rulers, supported by world powers, respond with utmost cruelty to crush the uprising, and even if a new regime survives the onslaught, it can be subverted to exercise centralized power, while the people fall back into patterns of internal division and subordination to authority. The response proposed by this manifesto is a global network of revolutionary collectives engaged in building grassroots democracy, to provide mutual aid (material, cultural, and moral) so that no one is left to meet repression in isolation, and to share lessons learned from victories and defeats: an inspiring call for internationalism from below!"

—**ROHINI HENSMAN**, author of *Indefensible: Democracy, Counterrevolution, and the Rhetoric of Anti-Imperialism*

"*Revolutions of Our Times* is a precious contribution to a truly internationalist mobilization against capitalism and imperialism. Such revolutionary voices are more than ever needed if we want humanity to survive."

—**MICHAEL LÖWY**, author of *Ecosocialism: A Radical Alternative to Capitalist Catastrophe*

"*Revolutions of Our Times* is a hard-hitting exploration of the challenges facing contemporary movements guided by emancipatory politics. Critical to twenty-first-century emancipatory politics is a recognition of the need to clarify the very notion of 'the people,' especially in highlighting the realities of marginalized populations for which global capitalism has little need. This volume also grapples with the entire notion of international solidarity of the oppressed in the twenty-first century, pushing the reader to appreciate the need for concrete assessments of actual conditions and the need to center our understandings on the struggles of the oppressed, rather than based on abstract geopolitics. This is a book I did not want to stop reading!"

—**Bill Fletcher Jr.**, trade unionist, author, and cofounder of the Black Radical Congress

revolutions of our times

AN INTERNATIONALIST MANIFESTO

Haymarket Books
Chicago, IL

© 2024 The Peoples Want

Published in 2026 by
Haymarket Books
P.O. Box 180165
Chicago, IL 60618
www.haymarketbooks.org

ISBN: 979-8-88890-590-6

Distributed to the trade in the US through Consortium Book Sales and Distribution (www.cbsd.com) and internationally through Ingram Publisher Services International (www.ingramcontent.com).

This book was published with the generous support of Lannan Foundation, Wallace Action Fund, and Marguerite Casey Foundation.

Special discounts are available for bulk purchases by organizations and institutions. Please email info@haymarketbooks.org for more information.

Cover design by Chantal Jahchan.

Printed in Canada by union labor.

Library of Congress Cataloging-in-Publication data is available. Library of Congress Control Number: 2025949184

10 9 8 7 6 5 4 3 2 1

contents

prologue	1
recognizing ourselves	4
birth of our power	9
finding the emergency brake	22
turning exile into a position of attack	35
internationalism from below	46
the fall of Empire	62
revolution?	77
starting over	96

Thailand 2013, 2020
Hong Kong 2014, 2019
Burma 2021
Sri Lanka 2022
Iran 2009, 2017, 2019, 2022
Bakur-Kurdistan 2015
Bangladesh 2024
Iraq 2019
South Korea 2016
Syria 2011
India 2019
Lebanon 2005, 2019
Bahrain 2011
Palestine 2000, 2005, 2020
Kyrgyzstan 2005, 2010, 2020
Yemen 2011
Kenya 2024
Kazakhstan 2022
Uganda 2024
Georgia 2003, 2024
Sudan 2013, 2018, 2019
Turkey 2013
Egypt 2011
Ukraine 2004, 2014
Greece 2008, 2011
Belarus 2006, 2020-2021
Libya 2011
France 2005, 2018, 2023
Tunisia 2011
Nigeria 2024
UK 2011
Algeria 2019
Burkina Faso 2014
Iceland 2008
Morocco 2011
Catalonia 2019
Senegal 2022-2023
Spain 2011
Kabylia 2001

Quebec 2012

USA 2011, 2014, 2015, 2020
Haiti 2019
Brazil 2013
Colombia 2021
Nicaragua 2018
Ecuador 2019

Peru 2009, 2022

Argentina 2001
Chile 2019

prologue

In autumn 2019, somewhere in the suburbs of Paris, people from all round the world came together to attend the first ever "The Peoples Want" gathering. Paris is a colonial metropolis, but it is also a crossroads, a place where for many centuries exiles have gathered. The name we gave of our meeting was intended as a tribute to a cry that shook the world for more than a decade: "The People Want the Downfall of the Regime." By swapping "Peoples" for People, we were expressing an aspiration.

A few years earlier, this rallying cry was brought to Paris in the luggage of Syrian revolutionaries. An encounter with local dissidents gave birth to a cooperative called "The Syrian Canteen." It was intended as a warm place in which to recoup strength and courage, where people could break out of their isolation, where the most intense debates revolved around food and revolution, and where, gradually, a community of exiles and friends from several countries was able to coalesce.

It was out of this community that "The Peoples Want" arose, as a series of transnational gatherings year after year attended by revolutionaries from all over the world. We shared our experiences and discussed what we were trying to build and fight for in our territories and neighborhoods. We took time to get to know each other over large banquets and parties, heard inspiring speeches, and participated in discussions that were sometimes difficult. Above all, we allowed ourselves to imagine that the future held possibilities beyond the repressive blanket of lead that had descended.

The last of these meetings set us on a new course. Revolutionaries from forty countries attended, and thousands of people came to meet them. Many expressed the desire to build something more sustainable, to go further. This energy proved that there was work to be done, that we were just at the beginning. So, the canteen remained a canteen, and the network began to draw its own constellation.

The process of writing this text began in the summer of 2023. It consisted of nine people from different parts of the world—Lebanon, France, Syria, Russia, Tunisia, Chile, Kurdistan, and Iran—coming together to establish a first draft. Nine contributors who, each in their own way, had taken part in the uprisings of our time. Different versions of this text were then offered for discussion from Santiago to Beirut, from Lyon to Buenos Aires, from the Massif

Central to the Galloway Hills via the Beqaa Valley. Along the way, it was debated, reworked, fleshed out, and in places changed entirely. From places of exile, from sites of struggle, North, South, East, and West, our words have been enriched by contributions from participants in the revolutions in Egypt, Sudan, and Iraq; the peasant revolts in India; the feminist wave in Latin America; the movement for George Floyd in the United States; the uprising in Sri Lanka; the Palestinian and Ukrainian resistance; and many others.

Putting ideological considerations aside, foregoing dominant discourses and TV studio geopolitics, we traveled to engage with bodies in struggle, then pooled our experiences. From these many encounters, and the illumination they produced, we tried to grasp what was at stake, and make the most of many uncertainties and apparent contradictions, to analyze forces at play and understand our most immediate challenges. We then set ourselves a series of short-, medium-, and long-term objectives. The intensification of open warfare—in Ukraine, Sudan, Palestine, and Lebanon, to mention only the most recent—and the reinforcement of the bloc logic this implies, seemed a major obstacle. How could we not appear out of step, when drawing up plans for a new internationalism, at a time when bombs were going off everywhere?

recognizing ourselves

Nos costó tanto encontrarnos, no nos soltemos[*]

The memories of our era are filled with images of its ongoing collapse: forests in flames, seas turned into graveyards, epidemics, famines, and murderous invasions . . .

But we could choose to remember something else. We could remember the power of the uprisings that shook the countryside and cities of the world, sparing no continent, no geography. Time and again, in the midst of this suffocating atmosphere of the end of civilization, people had risen against fatalism. Governments, regimes, and a few heads fell. People returned to knock on history's door.

Hundreds of police stations set on fire by protesters in Iran. A thousand public buildings attacked by rebels from working-class neighborhoods in France. Giant barricades on Maïdan in Kyiv, banks

---

[*] *It was so hard to find each other, let's never again be apart*

stormed by insurgents in Lebanon. Everywhere, violent insurrection offered a response to the violence of humiliation.

Those who lived through the ransacking of triumphal arches, the invasion of presidential swimming pools, or participated in furious dances echoing across borders remember the rage. The rage but also beauty liberated in defiance of sadness. We remember the warmth of a library built under siege, late-night conversations in improvised street kitchens, splendid walls adorned with slogans, words of wit and messages of love, those tens of thousands of voices singing in unison that nothing would ever be the same again.

Let them repaint the walls and remake their statues. They can send us into exile. They can lock us up and slaughter our people. A flame burns deep in our hearts through the hardest, coldest, most sinister moments.

In revolt, we have regained our dignity. From continent to continent, from our exile, in our travels and in our struggles, we have found each other. In the clash of street battles, gestures seen and then replicated in different countries, words echoed across languages, we have recognized each other. We understood that we belong to a single transnational struggle and that we stand against an internationally organized elite. We know that if we remain isolated, we will achieve nothing.

The bitterness of our defeats, and our refusal to accept them as final, has engendered the desire to get to know each other. We have begun to weave a network of planetary connections, from front lines to popular assemblies, from feminist strikes to resistance committees, from occupied roundabouts to occupied forests, and have discovered a common sensibility.

If the avant-gardes claimed to be marching one step ahead of the masses, we know that we are marching one step behind the popular uprisings of recent years. We have grown in their wake; they were our best school. Now we want to weave the fabric of a generational experience. By generation, we mean that which connects all those, regardless of age, gender, ethnicity, religion, or language, who have recognized the emergence of a new revolutionary cycle and felt a tremor in the depths of their hearts and bodies.

None of the ideologies, none of the political roadmaps we have inherited is capable of grasping the tumult of our times. We have not sought to create new ones. But we do have a notion of the method that will enable us to find paths together: It's called internationalism.

The revolutionary task has in part become a task of translation. Sharing and translating our different perceptions of reality, and circulating them, are the first steps in this method. This text is designed to highlight salient points of our first cross-analyses.

It attempts to organize them in a way that may be useful to anyone wishing to take an active part in what happens next.

Palestine (2000, 2005, 2019), Argentina (2001), Kabylia (2001), Georgia (2003, 2024), Lebanon (2005, 2019), France (2005, 2018, 2023), Iceland (2008), Iran (2009, 2017, 2019, 2022), Thailand (2013, 2020), Brazil (2013), South Korea (2016), UK (2011), USA (2011, 2014, 2015, 2020), Syria (2011), Morocco (2011), Libya (2011), Tunisia (2011), Spain (2011), Greece (2008, 2011), Egypt (2011), Sri Lanka (2022), Yemen (2011), Bahrain (2011), Quebec (2012), Turkey (2013), Ukraine (2004, 2014), Burkina Faso (2014), Bakur-Kurdistan (2015), Nicaragua (2018), Iraq (2019), Catalonia (2019), Ecuador (2019), Belarus (2006, 2020–2021), Kyrgyzstan (2005, 2010, 2020), Chile (2019), India (2019), Hong Kong (2014, 2019), Haiti (2019), Algeria (2019), Sudan (2013, 2018, 2019), Colombia (2021), Burma (2021), Kazakhstan (2022), Peru (2009, 2022), Senegal (2022–23), Bangladesh (2024), Kenya (2024), Uganda (2024), Nigeria (2024) . . .

This is not just an incomplete and unfinished list of the revolts of our time. Behind every place, behind every date, lie hundreds of thousands of faces, dreams, and lives. The following lines are a tribute to the insurgents who took part in these events; a tribute to those we have found, those we have yet to meet, and those we will never see again. To those who fell because they loved life. It is for our own sakes, but also for theirs, that we have decided to take to the road again; inspired by their presence and their energy. These words are dedicated to them.

birth of our power

THE MARGINS ATTACK THE CENTER | FROM THE MARGINS TO THE PEOPLE | THE FALL OF THE REGIME | THE PLAN WE MISSED

A fifteenth-century Arab thinker, watching his civilization crumble from bathing in superfluous luxury, worriedly predicted: The margins will put an end to Empire. What better image of this threat from the margins than Delhi in 2020, encircled by millions of peasants who had been long ignored. Peasants who, after the biggest strike in human history—a strike of 250 million people—set up peasant councils, the *Mahapanchayat*, all over the country saying, *The Mahapanchayat are the new parliaments of the people, and the untouchables will be at their center.*

the margins attack the center

As the uprisings of our time have shown, there is no global revolutionary subject. Black people in the United States, women and sexual and gender dissidents in Latin America, Baluchis or Kurds in Iran, indigenous peoples in Ecuador or Peru, youth from the working-class districts of Santiago and Tripoli. The revolt was led, above all, by those on the margins.

To be on the margins is to be part of the whole, but outside it. The margins include those who are carefully kept on the sidelines, not too far away to keep the machine running, but not too close to disturb; both outside and at the service of the centers. The centers are where power lies: state or capital city, multinational corporation, colonial settlers, bosses, patriarchs.

A revolt is limited when those who trigger it fail to rally other types of anger. Facing the centers, the great architects of our separation, the challenge of our uprisings was to ensure our encounter. Encounters between different segments of the margins, but also encounters between those on the margins and dissidents from the centers: those who defy the powers from which they benefit, such as the inhabitants of colonial metropolises who support liberation struggles in the colonies.

Where a segment of the margins, such as peasants in India, indigenous people in Ecuador, high school students in Chile, or black people in the United States, was joined by a large part of the population, uprisings have managed to achieve victories. Although these were often partial and provisional:

the withdrawal of reforms in India and Ecuador, the opening of the constituent process in Chile, and the pseudo-overhaul of several local police forces in the United States.

In an uprising, encounters between fighters from the margins and dissidents from the centers give rise to breaches that contain trenchant possibilities, where ambiguities and contradictions coexist. In the United States, the uprising triggered by the assassination of George Floyd was joined by white demonstrators in large numbers. After the first days of insurrection, these demonstrators tried to form a security cordon between the police and black insurgents in order to "protect" them. Without even realizing, they were helping to neutralize the anger and redraw racial boundaries that the insurrectionary movement had momentarily made less rigid. Nothing is a given in the encounter between dissidents from the centers and fighters from the margins—or between different sections of the margins themselves—but the moments of uprising were unique opportunities to shift the boundaries beyond compartmentalized milieus.

Where such encounters did not take place, the revolts multiplied in successive waves, but at a certain stage dispersed, fragmented, or were repressed. This was the case in Iran, where it was mainly the declassed middle classes who revolted in 2009, and working-class men in 2017 and 2019. It wasn't until 2022 that the regime faltered, when all components of society rose up behind women. In France, white dissidents of the centers didn't join the youth of working-class neighborhoods in 2005 or 2023, and the middle classes or unionized workers took little part in the Yellow Vest uprising of 2018. Without these encounters, regimes hold, governments buy time.

from the margins to the people

In the heart of Paris, during the insurrectionary evening of December 1, 2018, after breaking down the doors of the former Paris stock exchange, a black teenager, standing alongside a white protester in a yellow vest and an activist of Moroccan origin, enthusiastically blurts out, "It's us the people . . . Wallah (I swear on Allah), it's us the people!"

The revolt dismantles the separations produced by the centers, reconstituting the people. In Sudan, it was through meeting in the revolutionary processions of 2019 and at the sit-in in al-Qiyada Square that people from all parts of the country found themselves sharing their experience of the injustices that affected them all, although in different ways. It was in revolt that they first encountered each other, chanting together: "Unity is the people's choice!"

The uprising shatters the people that was constructed and rigidified by national novels, fascist ideologies, and dogmatic activists. Through their calls for unity, the margins of the uprising have often reinvented the people, in line with their own realities. That explains why, in France, a predominantly white movement like the Yellow Vests was so strong among colonized populations in Guadeloupe or Reunion; why a black woman, the son of a Portuguese immigrant, and a young Romani could be found among the movement's main leaders; why a small business owner and a working-class woman could hold a barricade together. In Sri Lanka, the 2022 uprising brought together, not without friction, Buddhist monks, queer people, Sinhalese, and Tamils, revealing the people for what they are: plural and in the making.

Weaving together the different fragments of the margins is done through speech as well as gestures. Syrian Arab revolutionaries understood this well when they used "azadi" (freedom), a word used in Kurdish, as a call to Kurds; the Turkmen of Iran when they sang "Kurdistan the eyes and light of Iran" to bring together historically antagonistic minorities; the use of the Mapuche flag in the 2019 demonstrations in Chile, and the Amazigh one in Algeria during the Hirak. In the heat of uprising, these gestures were all attempts to extend the people.

Yet, no segment of the margins is capable of unifying the diversity of people indefinitely. Unity is enabled by the sharing of experiences from the margins—insurrectionary practices, resistance in the face of repression, and the organization of immediate survival—more than by visions of change or ideological convictions. Whilst regimes were relentless in their efforts to divide the movement by all possible means, preexisting divisions also returned at the first opportunity, undermining the unity born of revolt. This leaves us with a major question: How can we maintain our unity beyond the peak of an uprising?

A people is always several things at once. It can be deceived, oppressed, participate in its own defeat or that of others. It can be divided, with each fragment fighting each other. But a people can also, on rare occasions, rally around a collective will to free itself from the political class that governs it. It's only through coming together, even if ephemerally, despite obstacles and contradictions, that the various segments of the margins, together with dissidents of the centers, have created a people with a new meaning. A people with revolutionary potential.

the fall of the regime

In Egypt, Tunisia, and Ukraine, regimes fell. In Lebanon, Sri Lanka, and Iraq, governments were overthrown. Yet even when movements seemed momentarily victorious, nowhere did the uprisings succeed in preventing a return to the established order or the arrival of the worst. Insurgents everywhere were painfully reminded that replacing a government or a constitution is not synonymous with threatening the powerful. The uprisings failed to reach the core of regimes.

An uprising is the eruption of the real movement, the self-assertion of those who have been pushed out of their humanity, dispossessed of their own strength. In this way, it signals both to the centers and to the margins themselves that the status quo can no longer continue. It fractures the legitimacy of established powers. The question remains, what to do with this fracture?

In 2022, Sri Lanka found itself on the verge of tipping over. Government buildings were occupied, the president had fled the country, and the army and police didn't dare intervene. In a way, revolutionaries had won the first round. But, hamstrung and outmaneuvered by institutional forces, not knowing what to do with the ministries, they returned them. As elsewhere, revolutionaries were beaten by the shock of their own victory.

In many uprisings, in the face of our inertia, politicians and technocrats of all stripes did not miss the opportunity offered by our weakness. The Muslim Brotherhood in Tunisia and Egypt, the military chiefs in Libya and Algeria, the "official" opposition of the Syrian National Council: The crowd of opportunists didn't wait for us to finish mourning our dead or nursing our wounded. While our barricades were still in place, they went to negotiate a "political outcome," synonymous with the end of the revolt.

How can we forget Boric, subsequently elected President of Chile, rushing into the halls of Congress in 2019, while the crowd was still confronting the police in the streets, to sign a biased agreement for a constitutional process to contain the revolt alongside the ruling political parties? As is so often the case, the institutional game intervened to restore order and prevent the country from plunging into the unknown. "If Piñera falls, we all fall," said a left-wing Chilean senator with lucidity. Politicians and bourgeois of both right and left always prefer to accept cosmetic change and a few concessions to ward off the advent of a revolution that would really threaten their power and wealth. To prevent a profound revolution.

During the Maïdan uprising in Kyiv in 2014, the ministry doors slammed shut once the regime was deposed by the street. Opposition parties were quick to propose a "transitional government," which they paraded on the central grandstand of the occupied square asserting their legitimacy. The insurgents were not fooled, but, after three months of insurrection, they were exhausted, and so the subterfuge came to pass. Insurgents thought they could keep a close eye on the new government and even proposed "people's" deputies. They pressured the new government by occupying a number of ministries to bring about institutional change and threatened to launch another Maïdan. But above all, it was a signal for everyone to go home.

In Sri Lanka, Chile, and Ukraine, for the uprising to have gone further, it would have been necessary to face the uncertainty of knowing how the country was going to feed itself, where to get fuel or medicine, or how to defend themselves against foreign military aggression. To know how to survive and live, rebels would have had to answer questions of scale that, for the moment, were beyond their grasp: what to do with state institutions, international organizations, the army, or foreign debt? How could they overcome obstacles without creating new dependencies? History has taught us that compromises often lead to concessions, i.e., variations of the same, rather than alternatives. So how do we keep fighting without falling into the abyss?

To do so, we need more than just material assurances. Throwing yourself into the unknown is an act of faith. It's done when there appears to be no choice. Or out of conviction, when you believe in something so deeply that it seems worth the risk. But what exactly do we believe in? What is our response to uncertainty? The days when socialism was on the table for every uprising are over. Without a map or compass, rebels have thrown themselves into the arms of those who had a plan: the reactionaries, the liberals, or the military. And those of us who ignited the revolt were left to contemplate, comment, and criticize—at least those of us who were still free, or alive.

the plan we missed
The irony is that perhaps the plan was there all along, right before our eyes.

Much has been said about the horizontal, decentralized nature of our revolts. About the extent to which the big traditional organizations were absent or incapable of monopolizing the "leadership" of the emerging movements. Leftists around the world appeared overwhelmed by the intensity and inventiveness of this wave of uprisings.

As a result, each uprising, each struggle, saw the emergence, independently of the directives of this or that leader, party, or organization, of new forms of popular organization adapted to the needs of each revolt. Occupations of squares, buildings, or universities in Greece, Egypt, Lebanon, Iraq, Sri Lanka, and Hong Kong; local councils in Syria and resistance committees in Sudan; territorial assemblies in Chile and Colombia; feminist assemblies around the world; roundabouts taken over by Yellow Vests in France.

In each of these experiences, insurgents found themselves organizing the offensive as well as the day-to-day life of the uprising. Assemblies were held to discuss strategy and prepare for highway blockades, demonstrations, and assaults on centers of power. We tried to organize security and self-defense, geolocated repressive forces, prepared legal defenses, and took care of the wounded. We built camps and shacks, fed crowds through *ollas communes* (popular kitchens), and occupied and cultivated vegetable gardens. Everywhere, we tried to ensure the proliferation of our forces and our possibilities for action.

In Syria, revolutionaries went even further. In territories from which the regime was ousted, insurgents managed to run entire towns, hospitals, mills, and power stations and distribute food by themselves for several years. The hundreds of local councils in the liberated territories were testimony to the fact that Syria's future lay neither in the hands of the National Council (opposition in exile), nor in those of armed groups. Yet revolutionaries didn't dare claim that it was they themselves who might actually be building an alternative to the regime. It was the demonstration in deed that even under bombs and siege, cut off from the world and facing ruthless repression, people were capable of taking the situation into their own hands.

In an uprising, we'll always face forces who won't hesitate to take over the palaces. And their priority will always be to defeat nascent forms of popular organization. Not being recognized as serious or legitimate by national and international forces, rebels were sidelined. Faced with these threats, we generally failed to influence the outcome of revolts. We were either unable or unwilling to take charge of the aftermath of the uprising. We failed to establish ourselves as a *power*.

In Sudan too, during the last decade of struggle (2013–present), resistance committees were set up in cities and neighborhoods. They organized both mobilizations and popular mutual aid. Year after year, revolt after revolt, they've grown in strength and experience. Following the ousting of President Omar al-Bashir, some opposition organizations decided to participate in the civilian-military Transitional Council. The resistance committees largely opposed this decision in order to remain faithful to the revolution's demand to remove all powers linked to the military. As a result, they themselves embodied popular legitimacy. Freed from opposition organizations and strengthened by this legitimacy, the hundreds of committees drafted and then voted on a proposal for the country's future: the Charter for the Establishment of People's Authority. Only in Sudan did the movement's grassroots committees dare to claim revolutionary power. Elsewhere, one of the great errors was to have reduced the emerging popular powers to the means of the revolution, rather than a unique combination of its means and ends. As a prefiguration of a possible revolutionary future.

These experiments offer a wealth of lessons for revolutionaries; they join and update a long history of popular power. It's a history that no textbook mentions: that of the *comandos comunales* and *cordones industriales* in Chile (1970–73); the *quilombos* of Brazil (1550–present); the *sans-culottes* sections of the French Revolution (1789–93); the *caracoles* of Chiapas and the workers' councils of Russia and Bavaria (1905, 1918–19); the communes of Paris

(1871), Morelos (1913), and Kronstadt (1921). And many others.

We interpret what we've lived through as an ongoing era of insurrection. What some quickly dismissed as defeat, we see as the birth of a worldwide movement of revolt for dignity. We look our failures straight in the eye, and prepare ourselves for victories to come. Our starting point is all those places to which popular power has returned, sometimes ephemerally, sometimes more tenaciously, to give us back our strength.

finding the emergency brake

BEHIND EVERY FASCISM LIES A FAILED REVOLUTION | THE AGE OF EXHAUSTION | A STATE OF EMERGENCY IN EVERY STATE | FINDING THE HORIZON

The beginning of this decade underlines a simple but painful truth: As revolution progresses, so counterrevolution grows harsh.

Recent uprisings have shown that all regimes, whatever their nature, are radically out of step with popular aspirations. Unable to rekindle faith in their moribund projects, the first response of those in power was terror. The uprisings left martyrs, prisoners, and exiles in their wake. The militarization of territories and the criminalization of struggles intensifies, while enforced disappearance and torture multiplies. To add to the national horror, Russian, Iranian, French, and US generals flocked to the bedsides of threatened regimes. Tear gas, bombs, and "French policing expertise" were offered to Ben Ali,

German policemen and Israeli cybersecurity systems to Chile, Iranian militias and Russian bombs to the aid of Bashar al-Assad. The crushing of our uprisings was not just national, it was international.

After the uprisings, what survives, gains strength, and even organizes itself is, more often than not, some form of reaction. Everywhere, the ruling classes fiercely defend their interests, whatever the cost. Across the globe, the only organized forces that seem to outlive the uprisings are conservative at best, fascist at worst. The last decade's uprisings have been brought to a halt by a large-scale and multifaceted response: a violent counterrevolution.

behind every fascism lies a failed revolution

Counterrevolution is not just a global counterinsurgency operation. Nor is it simply a restoration, a return to the old regime or the reestablishment of a social order battered by conflict and revolt. It actively builds a new order to suit its own needs. It shapes mentalities, cultural behaviors, tastes, habits, and customs. But there's more: Counterrevolution uses the same presuppositions and tendencies as those on which the revolution is based; it occupies the terrain of its adversary and gives other answers to the same questions. It reinterprets the revolution in its own way.

As revolutionaries are crushed, dispersed, and isolated, the heads of the hydra we thought we'd cut off slowly grow back. Whether through the decolonial costumes worn by Putin or Xi Jinping, the "anti-establishment" rebellions of Trump, Milei, or Bolsonaro, or the "free world's" war for "democracy," elites everywhere try to harness aspirations of the uprisings to prevent their return. In Argentina, the "*Afuera!*" (Out!) of Milei echoes the "*Que se vayan todos!*" (Out with them all!) of the rebels at the turn of the century. The best way to crush the desire for freedom is to present oneself as a liberator.

In 2024, Donald Trump participates in rallies featuring slogans such as "be ungovernable" and "mass deportation now." If fascists are our sworn enemies, it's not just because their project is the opposite of ours. They're our sworn enemies because they defend their project in revolutionary disguise, feeding off the impulses and aspirations of popular revolt while being the last resort of the centers. Putin, Meloni, Le Pen, like so many others, take advantage of the frustration and humiliation of the working class, undermined by the latest changes in capital, to consolidate their anti-establishment stance, so as to better defend the system. They claim to want to change everything so that nothing changes. Today, reactionaries are becoming more radical, while progressives flounder in moderation.

It's no coincidence that fascists have so much hatred for the feminist and queer movements. Fascism sees them as an adversary capable of creating a desire for liberation that could potentially threaten the established order. Feminists in the Global South have convinced millions to join their movements, thanks to their radical claim to empowerment and a will to change *everything* by transgressing the rules of gender, class, geography, and age. The same is true of the queer movement, one of the few that continues to dare to dream. By shattering the binary logic at the basis of all power, they turn the imaginary into a weapon, and desire into a force. By putting the body at the heart of transformation, the queer revolution is one of the few movements to stand in the way of the fascists' vision and embody possible futures. But, like so many other movements before them, they are being courted by the progressive factions of Empire, who are trying to defuse them and transform them into a harmless cultural accessory.

How can we believe that the bulldozing supremacisms of Trump, Modi, or Netanyahu could be beaten by a well-sourced argument, an Intergovernmental Panel on Climate Change (IPCC) report, the fact-checking of *The New York Times*, or a vote at the UN? Every time it ventures onto this terrain, progressivism is a little more mocked, a little more discredited, and therefore counterproductive. The resignation of social-democrats who claim it's impossible to change anything, even after winning elections, prepares the path for subversion by fascist forces who only have to stoop to harvest the legitimate anger and lost souls of the uprisings. From Washington to Brasília, so far, there has been nothing more than parodies of insurrection. The next time it could be much more serious.

The worldwide resurgence of xenophobic nationalism and the systematic attacks on women's rights and sexual and gender dissidence are the result of a well-planned global offensive, that of a neofascist international. The increasingly tense and grimacing faces of power may differ in appearance, yet they all belong to the same beast. For beyond their apparent conflicts and enmities, these forces share a common goal: to maintain the power of the centers, no matter the cost. To achieve this, no massacre will be too costly. On the contrary, war has always been the method of choice to keep revolution at bay.

the age of exhaustion

Everywhere, we have fallen into a state of emergency. Of all the regimes whose demise we could wish for, it is one of the most tenacious and multiform. It is indelibly inscribed even in our ways of organization and methods of struggle.

There are the immediate emergencies that spur us to action because it's no longer possible to endure things as they are. Not having enough to eat, risking death or rape on every street corner, finding nowhere to shelter oneself and one's children for the night, risking humiliation with every new administrative procedure, being beaten up at every identity check, fearing that there won't be enough water to grow crops, that the earth will turn to sand . . .

The precarity of life plunges us into a grueling daily routine, filled with imperatives that we can't even begin to resolve, and then another pressing situation arises. These emergencies, which unite us in our lived realities and monopolize our time and energy, are either faced alone or within our networks of relations, which are also exhausted. These daily pressures force us into unsustainable rhythms to keep struggles alive, to protect ourselves or avoid being crushed, demanding ever more energy simply to *exist*.

On the government side, as a cynical response to the emergencies just mentioned, there are those emergencies that, each in their own way, aim to remind us how helpless we are without the state's protection: "economic crisis," "'natural' disasters," "foreign agents," "external threats," "migratory crisis," and so on. The "State of Emergency" is utilized by all regimes, from the most democratic to the most despotic, as a measure of exception to the state of "peace."

The "emergency law" (Qanun al-Tawari') governed the daily life of Syrians for over forty years before the revolution. Officially put in place to counter the military threat of Israel, it has always been used to repress any internal dissent. A few months after the start of the uprising, it was transformed into the "counterterrorism law" but was still used to target any opposition. In Chile, the State of Emergency allowed President Piñera to (re)deploy the military against people in revolt. Over the last two decades, the use of the State of Emergency—as a legal justification for the absence of the rule of law—has spread everywhere, ostensibly in response to terrorist attacks as well as viruses, urban riots, and natural disasters.

a State of Emergency in every state

If politics is the continuation of war by other means, then governing and waging war are two sides of the same coin. The nation-state, with its particular way of structuring power, population management, and territorial control, has conquered almost the entire globe, through wars of colonization. However, the way in which power is exercised and populations controlled is not the same from one state to another, or from one region of the world to another.

The operation of the state apparatus is different for a former colonial power well established on the wealth it extorted from the rest of the world, than for a recently decolonized state under the influence of greater powers seeking to gain control over its resources. The degree of violence inflicted by the state on its own population is determined by the material means (colonial rent, oil rent, financial windfalls of various kinds) that the national elites have at their disposal to buy social peace before resorting to brute force.

Socialism, the welfare state, and social democracy, where they exist, have all been attempts to link the question of the state and that of popular sovereignty in a different way. In addition to its monopoly on "legitimate violence" and territorial defense, the state is also entrusted with the welfare of citizens, redistributing a part of the wealth, and providing services to the population. Each of these attempts, whether the outcome of revolutionary uprisings or reformist efforts, resulted in broadening popular support for the stability of the state.

But the time for social utopias is well and truly over. Hardly anyone is trying to sell us a rosy future. Dystopias have replaced utopias everywhere. There's the conspiratorial threat of the "Great Replacement" espoused by white racists; the society of control under the subordination of authoritarian artificial intelligences; the imminent collapse of living conditions on Earth. When the traditional parties of the left attempt to *reenchant* us with dusted-off political programs and new promises of change, it is now only due to the cyclical urgency of preventing the far right gaining power.

The "War on Terror" launched by the United States ushered in the twenty-first century. The pretext of the diffuse, omnipresent, and ever-imminent threat of *terrorism* has justified every war, every control measure, and every measure of exception at home and abroad. Mexico's "war on drugs," Russia's "denazification of Ukraine," Israel's "eradication of Hamas," Syria's "annihilation of the Zionist-Wahabi conspiracy," Turkey's "crushing of Kurdish terrorism," Mali's "ending Tuareg secessionism," Chile's "dismantling of Mapuche terrorism," and so many others . . . These are just some of the ways in which threats—some real, some fabricated—are used to divert societal tensions toward the fight against a common "enemy," the ultimate guarantor of national unity. A domestic protest that is a little too strong will quickly slip into the rank of "enemy from within" if it is not satisfied with the negotiating framework it's granted. The state is always portrayed as a "besieged castle," under threat from hostile forces within or on its doorstep. It is legitimized by the very thing that threatens it.

The emergency defines our relationship to the world and ushers in differing degrees of authoritarian methods to deal with disasters. In turn summoned by political forces, trade unions, and associations, then by governments that sometimes take them on board without responding to them, emergency has become the universal motif of politics. The only way to govern, or do activist work (where possible), is in the name of emergency. This imperative masks difference, conflict, and inequality: We are all concerned, in the same boat, equally victims, equally responsible, equally mobilizable.

Responding to a "social emergency," calling for a "state of ecological emergency," running from one cause to another, from a fight against an ecocide project to mobilization against a state reform, from a humanitarian crisis to an antifascist campaign. Each of these struggles, however important, sucks up all our available energy, and, lacking an overall strategy, we run around like headless chickens.

finding the horizon

The militarization of cities, swift border closures, the explosion of police controls, electronic surveillance and restrictions on movement, house arrests, and the management of the COVID-19 pandemic demonstrate that authoritarian measures are perfectly feasible on a large scale and over a long period of time. All that is needed to reactivate them when necessary is a well-crafted argument or crisis.

For a number of years now, things that haven't previously been in the media spotlight have been making headlines on 24-hour news channels: the sterilization of the oceans, the Australian or Amazon forests in the grip of flames, hurricanes and devastating floods. The mismatch between the positions and actions of governments and the proven gravity of the situation is clear to everyone. "Eco-anxiety" has become the disease of an epoch for those privileged enough not to have more pressing reasons to worry. It's another contributing factor to the general inertia. When we hear about wars, famines, humanitarian disasters, or mega-fires all day long, we're left in a daze. It's understandable, in order to survive, to ignore this information and carry on with life. As we are reminded of our own powerlessness, we are once again condemned to rely on an improbable leap of faith from the planet's leaders, or at least try to pressure them.

The very real ecological emergency is undoubtedly a powerful mobilizing force when concrete targets are identified and action strategies drawn up. The call to respond to the climate emergency is partly used by people fighting to defend their territories, by political organizations and environmental movements to gain attention and increase their forces, to legitimize more radical forms of mobilization and create unprecedented popular convergences. But as these emergencies become more widely recognized and threaten the interests of the ruling classes, leverage may well change hands. Ecology, for example, has already permeated right-wing and liberal political discourse, and the moment is fast approaching when talk of ecological collapse will justify a new authoritarian turn, Chinese Communist Party–style.

The youth of the centers are mesmerized by the prospect of their own tragic future, while those on the margins dream of plausible futures, with their back to the wall of an untenable present. The result is a repeatedly renewed disconnect between respective situations. In the time we have left, it is up to us to come up with a fresh response.

We must reestablish our own timeframe. We must make space to think together and apply the emergency brake. Whether we are living in a society already collapsing under the impact of war, natural disaster, or economic meltdown—or whether we belong to the heart of a Western fortress, stifled and haunted by the prospect of its forthcoming collapse—the only way forward is to elaborate a common plan, effective in each of our situations. And to ask:

What is the nature of this emergency? What leverage does it allow? What energy does it provide, what energy does it drain? What is to be gained in the race to define the root cause and nature of the emergency? What excessive means may it one day cause our opponents to use?

"Emergency," as a mandate to act, is a maneuver to win people over, and make them submit to an agenda. And, there can be little doubt as to who will have the means to win in the end. As far as popular movements are concerned, urgency is always a prelude to scattering and exhaustion. We need to focus, measure our actions and strike where striking can make a difference. Whatever the imperatives, whatever the pressure that can seem to immobilize us, the challenge is to act by focusing our energy and avoiding exhaustion. Organizing in the face of a counterrevolutionary offensive on this scale means rediscovering a horizon and building, for the long term: establishing connections and marshalling strength to avoid defeat in the insurrectionary explosions to come.

turning exile into a position of attack

DEADLY PATHS | ARRIVAL IN THE HOST COUNTRY | INCREASING CIRCULATIONS

Every attempt at revolution, every insurrection, leaves in its wake a new generation of exiled revolutionaries. In Cairo, Baghdad, Santiago, and elsewhere, uprisings have left people unable to return to their former lives, not only because of the existential upheaval experienced but also because of the cost of struggle. Losing an uprising is never without consequences. In addition to defeat, rebels pay the price through trauma, prison, mutilation, or death. Others experience the heartbreak of having to abandon their land and their loved ones. Our decade of uprisings has thrown a whole generation of Syrians, Sudanese, Iranians, Haitians, and Hong Kongers into exile, joining the Kurds, Palestinians, and Tamils of previous generations.

Exile is not just the result of political repression. An exile is also a person forced to abandon their homeland in order to survive, because home has become too dangerous, life has become unbearably expensive and the land less nourishing. Wanting a future for one's children, needing to live one's convictions or one's sexuality elsewhere are all causes of exile. For people on the margins, especially in the Global South, countless threats make staying at home too great a risk. Yet, the "migration crisis" has only just begun. Global warming will lead to massive displacement in the decades to come, as resources become increasingly scarce and large parts of the globe become uninhabitable. Paradoxically, the proliferation of borders and classifications on arrival only reinforce the desire to leave, rather than discouraging it.

Faced with domination, exploitation, and humiliation, we have three options: survive, flee, or revolt. Whether in Senegal, Haiti, or Lebanon, popular anger is multiplying at the same rate as departures. The clear-cut distinctions between "economic" migrants, "political" exiles, and soon-to-be "climate" refugees makes sense only to governments.

Revolt and exile are different responses to problems that have the same root: the exponential deterioration of living conditions and the proliferation of repressive regimes. Since the beginning of this century, people all over the world have been rising against those responsible for their material and emotional misery. Global and local elites, whether authoritarian or liberal, are obsessed with maintaining their power and wealth, always obtained through the endless exploitation of resources and the bodies of those living on the margins. Is it any wonder then that these populations try to reach the centers—to reclaim what has been plundered?

deadly paths

When we decide, or are forced, to leave our homelands, a new struggle begins. The roads of exile become more hostile by the day. The sea cemeteries of the Mediterranean or the English Channel, the death roads linking Latin America to the United States, the harsh desert of the Sahara that many African migrants cross only to risk enslavement in Libya. Exile is deadly, and like uprisings, it constitutes an act of refusal. You revolt or you leave, and sometimes you revolt and then you leave because you can't or won't put up with what you are put through. We flee because, despite the risks, sometimes flight is the safest option.

Governments continue to do everything they can to prevent "undesirable" migration: reinforcing security and military powers, increasing restrictions on freedom of movement, building walls and impenetrable borders, criminalizing solidarity with people on the move. Fortress Europe has established a specialized agency, Frontex, to keep those of us who have taken to the sea out of Schengen waters. States are quick to cooperate on these issues. Through lucrative agreements, Europe and the United States are trying to outsource border controls to Turkey, African countries, or Mexico so governments there may be seen to be "turning off the tap" of migration.

One hundred million Euros promised to Tunisia, in a state of economic collapse, by the European Union to "prevent illegal migration." First results: black people violently expelled from Tunisian territory to wander and die in a no-man's land in the middle of the desert. President Kais Saied has even borrowed the "Great Replacement" theory from the European far right. This conspiracy theory postulates that white, "native" European civilization is being demographically and culturally replaced by the massive arrival of non-white migrants, particularly Muslims. Saied's version turns this fable against black migrants, who are accused of changing the demographic and cultural makeup of Tunisia. Through constant repetition, this discourse has become entrenched in a society with its own history of racism. We've seen mobs attacking black people and demanding their expulsion.

In Sudan, the European Union has directly financed General Hemedti's *Janjaweed* Rapid Support Forces to "curb immigration." This paramilitary force, which was involved in the repression of the revolution and then went to war against the

Sudanese Armed Forces, had previously carried out ethnic cleansing operations in Darfur thanks to this funding. Since 2018, repression and the war have displaced more than 10 million people inside and outside the country.

To maintain a semblance of alignment with their humanist principles, European democracies externalize, meaning make invisible, some of the violence they are prepared to wreak against us. Violence is exercised internally and without restraint in urban ghettos on the fringes of metropolises. It is financed externally in the form of bloody repression abroad. The British government attempted to introduce a policy of deporting asylum seekers to Rwanda, in order to "deter unauthorized migration" by creating a "hostile environment" on British soil. Europe could not have been "enlightened" without being colonial.

Faced with this institutionalized xenophobic offensive, we must scale up our actions at borders to offer safe passage. In Europe, an autonomous maritime coordination system has been set up to organize solidarity in the Mediterranean: rescue boats at sea, telephone helplines, negotiations with the authorities, and public mobilization . . . Where such networks exist, we need to increase their capacity. Where they do not, we need to establish them. One of our main challenges is to ensure that comrades no longer die on the road to exile by providing efficient logistical support along major routes. We pay tribute to all those who have died on the road, to escape persecution, or simply in search for a dignified life.

But solidarity with those in exile is not enough. Freedom of movement is not limited to safe-passage or "legalizing" migration. Freedom of movement is meaningless if it does not imply the possibility of staying at home or returning. Hence the need to fight for a dignified life everywhere, instead of letting certain states claim to embody *the good life* while destroying the conditions that make it possible elsewhere.

arrival in the host country

The ordeal does not stop at the end of the road. As soon as we arrive in the "host country," we are confronted with the need to become "legal." A series of bureaucratic procedures are responsible for determining whether a person had enough reason to leave their country of origin, has enough money, or has a certain level of education or "talent" to be allowed to stay on the territory. Then begins a long process of classification and interrogation, an administrative limbo suffused with daily humiliation. Some eventually pass the test, others are rejected and deported as "illegals." The administrative battle is compounded by the material question: again, a struggle for decent living conditions, the need to find a roof over your head and a source of income, while learning a new language, new cultural norms, and new ways of doing things.

Those fleeing political persecution will not necessarily find security in exile. If they are not criminalized again for political activities, like Kurdish or Uyghur activists in Turkey, they may be threatened abroad, or even murdered, as was Rouhollah Zam, an Iranian activist living in exile in France, who was kidnapped in Iraq and then executed in Iran. The Chinese authorities have even set up clandestine police stations in Europe and the United States to exert their control over Chinese people abroad. In Britian, anti–Chinese Communist Party activism on campuses is muzzled by the threat of reduced investment in universities run like businesses.

In addition to government and police repression, many of us face an increasingly hostile local population in our places of exile. Elections everywhere are held against a backdrop of xenophobic media coverage, where racism and Islamophobia feature with increasing prominence. "Moderate" forces are beginning to speak the same language of reactionary politics in the hope of not losing ground. Depicting foreigners as a threat, as one of the main reasons for the deterioration in living conditions, is designed to channel citizen anger and anguish. Designating scapegoats is a very convenient strategy for those in power. It justifies growing inequalities, boosting the profits of the richest while absolving them of responsibility for the impoverishment of everyone else. In a sign of the times, in mid-summer 2024, coordinated white racist riots rocked towns and cities across England. Rioters targeted non-white people, Muslim places of worship, and hotels housing asylum seekers when a news story was successfully exploited by far-right networks. Only poor immigrants are called "aliens."

Xenophobia can also be more subtle. Racial discrimination is not just a flaw in state institutions, it affects everyone. Though we may receive compassion or sympathy in exile, we are generally denied a political role, as we were in the country we have had to leave. There is no shortage of curious people in the West who find our culture, our music, our food, our language "delicious" and "utterly fascinating," but who couldn't care less about our opinions on the way the world works. An exile is a humanitarian and depoliticized figure who arouses the charity and good conscience of left-wing citizens, and a folkloric object on which to project fantasies of elsewhere. "Multiculturalism," lauded in the age of globalization, is the analgesic for the destruction of cultures and worlds.

Antiracist circles and movements of solidarity with exiles are not exempt from these phenomena. Our analyses and involvement in movements in our countries of origin arouse little interest. For the most part we remain *outsiders*. The persistent ignorance of certain "comrades" we meet in exile, of the situations of struggle outside their national and psychic borders, is a form of paternalism that reduces us to the role of victims: the "economic crisis" in

Sri Lanka, the "civil war" in Syria or Sudan, or the Taliban in Afghanistan. This denial of our subjectivity and agency, combined with difficult material conditions, is a major obstacle to genuine political friendships. It creates a heap of missed opportunities that prolongs the ordeal of revolutionaries in exile and deprives local communities of the lessons, experience, and know-how that could only strengthen local militant activism.

In Greece, despite the economic crisis, the outpouring of solidarity with refugees led to a general mobilization of anarchists and revolutionaries. Squats, based on the principles of mutual aid, were opened in the cities to provide safe living spaces. They offered better living conditions and greater autonomy than government camps. Collective kitchens were established, and practical support given to help meet basic needs (clothing, language courses, and access to job opportunities) as well as access to physical, mental, and reproductive health care. Exiles and their supporters worked together to ensure self-defense against attacks by fascists and the state. Within a few years though, exhaustion set in; with a lack of horizon and sometimes common goals, and due to the gentrification policies of some neighborhoods, the movement lost its momentum.

Our primary task is to create and connect places of refuge to ensure the humanitarian minimum. We also need to consolidate lasting structures to generate new energy, heal trauma, reduce loneliness, and ensure subsistence. To do all this, we first need to meet each other.

increasing circulations

Internationalism, like revolutionary theory, has always been closely linked to exile and diasporas. Throughout history, many revolutionaries have, at one time or another in their life, had to abandon their country of origin. They have been deported; they have had to migrate; they have been forced into exile; they have wanted to join a guerrilla movement. They have encountered new realities, familiarized themselves with different contexts, and shared analyses of the events that shook the countries they left behind. Far from being a mere coincidence, the transnational mobility of these figures was fundamental to nourishing practice and disseminating thought.

Internationalism is a journey, not only of people but also of ideas and practices. Thinking about exile is a response to the challenge of constructing common perceptions despite a diversity of local contexts and the specific difficulties inherent to different situations. Exile can be experienced as an extension of revolt, a bridge linking it to the rest of the world. This could prove a means of compensating for the profound lack of understanding that many of today's revolts have faced, due to the lack of relations between revolutionaries from different parts of the world.

Despite the daily struggle for regularization and dignified living conditions, despite the priority we logically give to solidarity with the struggle in our home countries, we need to link up with local and diasporic liberation forces wherever we arrive. In Berlin, a whole generation of exiles and their allies are organizing joint demonstrations for the liberation of Palestine, Syria, Ukraine, Iran, and Sudan. It is from this united front between foreigners that exiled people feel powerful, no longer isolated, each in their own "minority" and "marginal" struggle.

Participating in (or initiating) local mobilizations as exiles, and forging alliances with the forces at work, could well prove to be the best way to take up the offensive with new levers, more allies, and new horizons. The links between revolutionaries from different geographies, which are easier to forge in exile, help to increase material and political support for our comrades and loved ones still on the front lines or under the bombs.

Building a force capable of coordinating and supporting revolutionary efforts wherever they arise will involve a struggle to bring together a generation of defeated and exiled people scattered across the globe. It must respond to defeat, exhaustion, and dispossession materially and emotionally. But it must also offer a more powerful remedy: the preparation of a response.

internationalism from below

THE PROBLEM OF "SOLIDARITY" | MUTUAL AID | EXTENDING THE *MINGA* WORLDWIDE | DOWN WITH REALPOLITIK, FOR A REVOLUTIONARY TENDERNESS

Although everything has been done to belittle the power of people in revolt, its impact has proved contagious. No amount of attempting to disrupt communication between different struggles has succeeded, no amount of trying to blur their meaning. Hope, courage, and insurrection have crossed bodies, territories, and all borders. The death of a Tunisian street vendor in December 2010 triggered one of the biggest revolutionary waves in history. When Lebanese people chanted *Kilon yani Kilon*,* this was a belated reference to an Argentinian slogan at the start of the century, *Que Se Vayan Todos*,** and also

---

* "Every Single One Means Every Single One"
** "Out with Them All"

to Tunisians' chanting *Dégage*.* Feminists the world over chanted *Jin, Jiyan, Azadi*.** Protesters in Brussels and Lausanne took to the streets after the murder of Nahel by French police. Colombian front lines borrowed their shields and their chants from the frontlines of Chile. By challenging the mirage of nation-states, twenty-first-century rebels realized they were fighting a common enemy. Same cops ahead, same banks behind, same bastards on top.

Feeling is not enough. It does not make for a front. Rebellious Egyptians proved unable to send cordons of "ultras" to support the uprising in Libya. Communalists the world over failed to give support to local councils in Syria. The Zapatistas lacked the means to send experienced cadres to front lines in Chile and Colombia. Anonymous hackers alone have been plugging the gaps, attacking digital strongholds round the world in support of rebels.

The absence of support from revolutionary forces led Syrian rebels to accept arms and funding from Saudi Arabia and Turkey. The Palestinian resistance is forced to take money from Iran and Qatar. The Kurds of the PYD (Partiya Yekîtiya Demokrat, or Democratic Union Party) are dependent on the Assad regime and have sought help both from its Russian ally and the United States in order to survive. Revolts in West Africa are relying on support

---

* "Out of Here"
** "Woman, Life, Freedom"

from Russia and China to oust France. Popular resistance in Ukraine has had to place its survival in the hands of the West.

Dependence on superpowers is a question of survival for many revolutionaries, so how can we condemn them? It's unreasonable to expect people to continue living under repression, capitulate, or wait passively as the bombs fall. A lack of international support condemns revolutionaries to isolation or the hijacking of popular demands by foreign powers more concerned with their own interests than those they claim to help. Syrian revolutionaries, abandoned by the whole world asked: "Governments have betrayed us. Where are the peoples?"

the problem of "solidarity"

In Iraq, after the US invasion had destroyed local seed banks, international organizations flooded the country with genetically modified seeds distributed to farmers free of charge. In order to use them, farmers had to purchase fertilizers and chemical pesticides from foreign companies, which meant that many fell into debt and were forced to abandon their land. This is how humanitarian aid prolonged colonial domination and led one of the cradles of agriculture to ruin.

Over the last few decades, "international aid" has come to replace internationalism, deemed too partisan and so sacrificed on the altar of "development." This approach has long been criticized for the hierarchical dependence it creates in Southern countries on Northern NGOs. Although humanitarian aid may save lives, it rarely tackles root causes. Band-aids don't stop the bleeding. Even where international aid terms itself "solidarity" and attempts to provide concrete solutions, the effects are often perverse.

In Palestine, the mass arrival of NGOs, foundations, and other international organizations followed the Oslo Accords. Popular self-organization that had grown out of the *intifadas* was diluted in "civil society," where resistance efforts were formalized, encouraged to become "projects" with logos, statements of intent, and budgets. By making funding conditional on "apolitical" actions, grassroots initiatives are disfigured and popular resistance is weakened. In any case, the Israeli occupying authorities exercise absolute control over any form of civil grouping in the West Bank and Jerusalem. So, it's hardly surprising that Hamas, a reactionary organization, concentrates all hopes for national liberation. These essentially top-down solidarities make aid conditional on rules and times that are disconnected from territorial struggles, as are the allegiances, codes, language, and bureaucracy they require.

To gain exterior support, a cause must be made acceptable, even attractive. Dependence on external funders subordinates a cause to the support it's likely to receive. Such a cause is often molded to obtain the greatest possible return and guarantee competitiveness on the solidarity market. Solidarity of this kind alters the spirit of a struggle and submits margins to centers, be they Western, Russian, Turkish, Chinese, or in the Gulf. Syrian revolutionary brigades had to either cut off their beards to obtain Western support, or grow them to get money from Qatar or Saudi Arabia.

Even when "international solidarity" organizations and collectives leave a great deal of autonomy to those in struggle and trust people on the ground, they often generate one-way relationships. In order to compensate for structural inequalities and the relationships of domination that they produce, common political and ethical lines as well as strategic practice need to be defined by the people concerned—those on the receiving end of solidarity and those handing it out. The aim is to create conditions conducive to mutual aid, based on equal relationships that acknowledge reciprocity between struggles and territories.

mutual aid

Mutual support begins with recognizing our need to work together. This is bound to be a gradual process. Making relationships truly reciprocal takes time. So does building bonds of trust. Both involve knowing how to be there for each other. Both demand erasing the distinction between word and deed. Rather than doing good deeds, the idea is taking other people's struggle into account as being a part of our own, and vice versa. In a world where competition reigns supreme, even between struggles, this is the reversal of a paradigm.

Mutual aid has no center because it operates in multiple directions, and acknowledges power relations. When the first workers' solidarity funds in the nineteenth century sent money to support a strike, they insisted that these were *loans* rather than donations. The idea was not to expect interest or even actual repayment. It rather asserted that help was not given out of kindness or charity but was a gesture that called forth others in return, at other times, or in other forms. It's clear that it's easier to send financial support from the Global North to the South than vice versa. But this is not the only form that mutual aid can take.

The first form of mutual aid is material. It takes us back to the *minga* (coming together for the common good). In Abya Yala, this principle is embodied in different ways by pooling the tasks, resources, and goods needed for collective work: helping to move a house, cultivating a field, constructing a building. It's when people, neighbors, and communities work together, but also take advantage of the moment to enjoy the conviviality of being together and building strong communal bonds. The uprisings and their aftermath have made visible the need for material aid, from medicines to seeds, involving a long chain of people and places. To do this, allies are needed who can open paths and cross borders. Solidarity convoys to collectives in Greece after 2008 and popular mutual aid initiatives to Ukraine since 2022 both constitute examples to be generalized, built on, and shared. There's considerable scope for progress in this area.

Such schemes need money. How can financial support, both popular and effective, be achieved? Or to put it another way: Is it possible to finance a revolution without the help of the powerful? Many diasporas, whether Kurdish, Palestinian, or Burmese, whether very recent or a long time ago, have helped struggles in their native countries survive. The Burmese resistance, for instance, popularized "revolutionary crowdfunding," raising hundreds of millions of dollars to finance resistance groups. Aggregating micro-contributions on a massive scale and setting up transnational mutual funds can both limit our dependence on the goodwill of patrons, governments, and NGOs.

Beyond the directly material question, mutual aid can take the form of amplifying the voices of individuals and groups grappling with the reality of the revolutionary terrain. The task of an international aid network is to help them break through the media net and the background noise of the reactionary communication channels. No revolution should ever again feel orphaned or betrayed by global indifference. This presupposes being able to communicate with people on the ground at crucial moments. It means obtaining information and translating it to suit other contexts. It involves coordinating support actions and establishing long-term communication channels to share our analyses.

It's vitally important to create a common history, weaving together all our accumulated experiences. This implies making the history of previous struggles and experiences known. Running an antifascist campaign, writing a feminist constitution, developing farming techniques, defeating an army of trolls, defending ourselves against the police, setting up funding networks, and answering daily needs within a liberated area are skills and knowledge that can be shared. Conservative and counterrevolutionary forces are doing everything they can to portray our uprisings as disasters, our rebels as terrorists, and our achievements as failures. The battle of narratives and images is more important than ever, both in the immediacy of the struggle and to nourish a memory of the future, as Chilean comrades say.

Mutual support may be embodied in action. It can mean blockading an arms factory to reduce bombings elsewhere, or disrupting a multinational corporation in one place to undermine extraction across the globe. It can also mean influencing what is known as "public opinion" where people live, work, and spend their leisure time in order to build support for those on front lines. Mutual aid is the driving force behind internationalism. By acquiring an international profile, local struggles develop a capacity for global action and create global alliances against borderless networks of power and money. We will not lack common enemies.

extending the *minga* worldwide

People will ask, "But there are already so many things to fight for and against here ... why add international struggles to the list? We need to avoid dispersion and exhaustion." The priority and urgency of local situations is always more pressing. It might even seem illusory to claim to be changing the situation elsewhere when we are struggling to do so where we are. Internationalism sometimes seems like a romantic dream, beautiful but basically naïve, like a relic from the past, a dusty box full of memories and postcards: Vietnam, Cuba, Algeria, Spain ...

But building internationalism has never been a luxury, it's a survival strategy. Those who have made it a pillar of their struggle (the Zapatistas, Kurds, Palestinians) are almost the only revolutionary movements to have survived long-term to the present day, despite relentless attacks from all sides. For these movements, internationalism has compensated for the imbalance of power between the grassroots and the military forces they face, has shifted the terrain of hostilities to the diplomatic level and created worldwide solidarity networks. In their time, the historic victories against colonialism in Ireland, Vietnam, and Algeria were won by insurgents on their own soil, but also through winning the hearts of the people in the center of empires, until the people of those countries themselves demanded an end to war and occupation. Fighting from the belly of the beast is always necessary to broaden the front and arena of confrontation and support those on the ground. But we need to listen to their demands, rather than centering ourselves and giving precedence to our own political positions or applying our own analytical framework to the situation.

While we draw on historical precedent, we're not nostalgic for some "golden age" of internationalism. In the twentieth century, internationalism was largely aligned with the interests of nation-states, and it fractured as a result. Instead of combating nationalism, it sometimes reinforced it. Attachment to land and culture as terrains of struggle has its place, but we should be wary of its instrumentalization by state apparatuses that serve national ruling classes. Internationalism begins at home, in our everyday territories. Places where populations are diverse, mixed, heterogeneous, and, strictly speaking, inter-national are fertile ground for it. These include the world's metropolises, border areas, and the major agricultural production zones that rely on immigrant labor. Internationalism means establishing multiple links between struggling peripheries, between different *corners of the world*, to reduce the attractiveness of regional and global centers of power.

Our territories are interwoven with transnational production logics. The power of a local political proposal today lies in its ability to see itself as part of a global network of resistance and uprisings. Without this, it runs the risk of being reduced to an "alternative" experiment, whether that is cultural, economic, or social, ignoring the links that tie it to the rest of the world. Conversely, unless firmly established at the local level, internationalism can be no more than a nostalgic song, or a nice meeting place for a cosmopolitan activist elite. The challenge we face is to extend the *minga* worldwide, between territories of struggle, between popular powers. This is what we mean by internationalism from below.

Looking at what's happening elsewhere is a breath of fresh air, giving us strength and courage when "home" becomes dark and unbearable. Somewhere on earth, there are always people who are organizing, who don't give up. Since 2011, while people have shown an awareness of other people's struggles and borrowed from them, intensifying exchanges, there is still no sign of a transnational revolutionary force capable of connecting resistance movements and revolutions without taking control of demands and aspirations. There is no time to lose in building such a force if we want to make a decisive impact.

down with realpolitik, for a revolutionary tendency

It won't always be easy to find common lines of defense and attack, even if we share the same desires and hopes. There are a multitude of obstacles ahead. We don't speak the same language; we live far apart; understanding local complexities takes time. Added to these practical difficulties is the posturing of those who actively oppose our struggles out of "pragmatism" or out of counterrevolutionary nonsense. Such are overarching, geopolitical approaches, reminiscent of a bad remake of the Cold War, minus the socialism. From this perspective, in the final analysis, world events are only ever determined by a clash of blocs. States are the only agents capable of affecting change. Anything that goes beyond the realm of realpolitik, and is therefore potentially revolutionary, is doomed to failure.

This binary logic has led a section of the "anti-imperialist" left to support, implicitly or explicitly, the Iranian, Russian, Chinese, and Syrian Assad regimes as "bulwarks" against imperialism, Zionism, colonialism, and Western-capitalist hegemony. According to this point of view, the Syrian and Iranian revolutions are seen as "liberal" or "pro-Western" and easily "manipulated." They were dismissed as plots hatched by foreign countries, obviously Western, to compromise the "national sovereignty" of the regimes in place. In this narrative, the people, their forms of organization, their autonomous actions, the plurality of their voices, their internal social or class struggles—like the massacres committed against them by these regimes and their allies—count for nothing.

These self-proclaimed "anti-imperialists" can seem so far out of step with real movements that when uprisings occur, they rush to apply their abstract interpretations, and deprive those most affected of their ability to make themselves heard. In their eyes, the popular resistance in Ukraine, the feminists in Iran, and the revolutionaries in Syria are either "agents of imperialism" or incapable of understanding their own situations. From their supposedly "critical distance" these ideologues, usually based in the West, believe they know better than people on the ground what needs to be done. When those in revolt put forward analyses and demands that don't fit with their dogma, resistance fighters in Ukraine are slandered as "Nazis," the rebels in Syria are called "jihadists," the feminists in Iran "traitors." This is what these "anti-imperialists" are doing, acting as proxies for the murderous regimes they support and defend.

Seeing Western countries as the only imperialist powers, and the United States as *the* source of all evil, a characteristic bias of these "campist" positions leads them to relativize the crimes of the Syrian, Russian, Chinese, or Iranian regimes. The maintenance of these regimes, or even their rise to prominence, would be opportune, according to this logic, to balance the world order and counter Western hegemony.

Imperial powers such as China and Russia, which rhetorically support the cause of Palestine, are seen as allies, or the lesser evil vis-à-vis the hypocrisy of Western countries, all aligned behind the Israeli colonization. But more "opportune" or "lesser evil" for whom? Why should we tolerate the genocide of Uyghurs in China in order to put an end to the genocide in Gaza? Why should we denounce the Israeli colonization of Palestine on one hand, and turn a blind eye to the counterinsurgency war in Chechnya, Russia's invasion of Georgia or Ukraine, and vice versa?

In 2019, Iraqi rebels, who have some experience of imperialism, made clear in mass demonstrations that they wanted "neither the USA nor Iran" in their country. There are subtle categories and more or less complex theoretical labels to describe the different types of imperialism that exist today, but "sub-imperialism" is the same old shit we've always known.

"Campist" positions only create barriers and divisions between struggles. They prevent necessary alliances between people on the margins. Instead of emphasizing what unites us, these "pragmatists" tell us that, to be effective, we should consider that the enemies of our enemies are our friends. Solidarity is therefore based less on what is happening on the ground than on the positions taken by the United States. If the United States supports a cause, such as the rebellion in Hong Kong, opportunistically, then the people of Hong Kong are undeserving of support, no matter how much China wants to extend its authoritarian grip there. This is a "Kissinger" and not a "Che Guevara" approach. It is ethically deplorable and strategically counterproductive: We need a revolutionary tenderness capable of listening, wanting to understand, navigating contradictions in order to stand alongside those in struggle. We are placing our bets on those who want to change the rules of the game, rather than on those who want to win the game as it is.

Contrary to what an authoritarian and statist left would have us believe, linking struggles increases our power. Building collective strength is exactly what the feminist movements in the southern part of Abya Yala managed to achieve in recent years. By taking into account multiple forms of violence—against sexual dissidents, Afro-descendants, women, indigenous people, migrants, children, the elderly, whether at work, in the street, at home, or by the police—and including all those impacted in the feminist general strikes, rather than seeing them as rivals, they succeeded in weaving together a huge popular movement. United but not uniform. Massive but radical.

Those who are too impatient or have no horizon of their own prefer to take refuge in the shadow of the powerful rather than share the fate of those who run the risk of being defeated. We must *fight against our own weakness*, and in particular against the belief that we can do nothing without participating in the games played by the powerful. Admittedly, we feel that we are few and that we are lacking in resources. But recognizing this and using it as a starting point to build our strength is certainly more realistic than taking shortcuts, clinging to second best, and thus reproducing the conditions of our powerlessness.

Only the people can save the people. We need to give substance to this slogan by starting to build, in the four corners of the globe, a transnational force capable of effectively countering the *cold monsters* that are devouring our present and future. Building a real force for intervention and mutual aid will take time and require resources that we need to patiently prepare, but it's the only way forward. No real victory is possible in just one part of the world. Empire has established itself everywhere, so it's only by confronting it everywhere, simultaneously, that we may one day share in its downfall.

the fall of Empire

WHAT WE MEAN BY "THE WEST" | EMPIRE WILL OUTLIVE THE WEST | "EACH GENERATION MUST, IN RELATIVE OBSCURITY, FACE UP TO ITS MISSION: FULFILL IT OR BETRAY IT" | STOPPING THIS WORLD

Across the planet, despite the walls and fences placed in their way, despite the many strategies of assimilation and annihilation, people are reclaiming territories, resources, cultures, and heritages. They're fighting for everything they've been robbed of by centuries of colonial plunder and imperial pretentions. Such is the case of the Palestinian resistance, which has held out against Israeli colonization and Western imperialism for over 70 years, or the Kurdish movement, which has been fighting for over a century against four nation-states that deny its right to autonomy. In Abya Yala, indigenous and Afro-descendant revolts have not ceased since 1492 and continue to inspire the continents' struggles. From Wounded Knee to Oka, from Standing Rock to the uprising for George Floyd, from the Mapuche resistance in Wallmapu to the defense of water in Cochabamba, people are rising up against a system of domination based on white supremacy and the exploitation of our bodies and territories. Time and again, revolts against racist police crime flare in Europe, while Kanaky continues its anticolonial struggle against France, and in West Africa French postcolonial authority continues to be dismantled.

But international waters are murky and disputed and are difficult for insurgents to navigate. Until now, the centers have kept a firm grip on the horizon, confining each struggle, each uprising, to its particular context. Dominant figures in the centers cannot believe that anyone would want anything other than to join the center. The center is the best of all possible worlds. The rest of us can only run to catch up, collapse, get up again, and hope one day to make it. The only world we have in common is the world as defined by the victors of "globalization." But when revolutionary irruption does occur, it gives rise to a different "world in common," which emerges from the ruins, cracks, and margins. This is the common world we need to name, born of revolt and free of the specifics of its various contexts.

what we mean by "the West"
The incredible claim of the West to define a "universal" horizon for humanity has caused and justified

millions of deaths, genocides, epistemicides, not to mention the enslavement and displacement of millions of people. What a macabre, an effective intellectual swindle! The founding myth of the "free subject" forged and propagated by the "Enlightenment" was born in the context of a revolutionary struggle against tyranny. It has been transformed, into an alibi for limitless expropriation under a new economic order, in lieu of the good word of God. The Universal Declaration of Human Rights was proclaimed with great fanfare the same year that the Palestinian *Nakba* (catastrophe) sent hundreds of thousands into exile.

Liberal "universalism" is the apolitical rival of internationalism. It preaches that human rights are inalienable, and denies them to most. It teaches that states belong to an "international community" where good relations between nations are harmonized. Yet, this is no more than a playground where hierarchies are masked and vassalages disguised. Words are bandied about, action and good resolutions are mimed, as if to conceal what everyone knows deep down: that the survival of the fittest still governs the human world.

The "international community" is a private club of nation-states, in which hegemons agree on criteria for membership, while justifying perpetual dominion over those who don't fit the bill. The latter are not exactly "excluded": They are afforded a sort of partial membership. *Some are more equal than others.* And it's the same with these entities' populations: Some are deemed human, some are human shields, some are human animals, and some just collateral damage. The United States invaded Afghanistan and also Iraq. It bombed many parts of the Middle East, at a cost of more than a million lives, in the name of "protecting democracy" and the "universal ideal of human rights." Even as we write these lines, an Israeli colonial state is knowingly committing genocide in Palestine with the blessing of the West, and occupation troops sometimes fly the LGBTQI flag.

Yet Empire's cynical use of the garb of "human rights" to establish itself as a universal judge of peace has not prevented "human rights" also being claimed as a discourse of resistance and a basis of support for popular struggles throughout the world. There is therefore a contradictory dual use of international law, by the centers and by the margins. Indigenous or colonized peoples regularly use the "right to self-determination" as leverage in their struggle against their national governments and occupying forces. Human rights and their symbolic weight on the international stage regularly serve as a reference point for resistance to oppression on the ground, as a denunciation of state terrorism. But the lightning rod of international law offers little protection if it does not serve the interests of dominant powers. They will always prefer to turn a blind eye when the price is not worth it. So it was with the red lines of the "free world" on the use of chemical weapons by the Assad regime against its own population. The people of Ghouta were expendable.

NATO's "humanitarian" or "responsibility to protect" intervention, which took place in Libya during the 2011 uprising, is one of the key events in this latest revolutionary sequence that nobody is talking about anymore. The end of a local order, through the intervention of advocates of a "global order," interrupted the revolutionary process and created new dependencies. The Anglo-French intervention, while likely to have prevented a bloody Syrian-style scenario, has enabled the establishment of a semblance of governments that are not born of revolutionary spaces, yet possess a right to sign agreements on behalf of people who asked for nothing of the kind. The Libyan revolution has thus been lost in internal power struggles between factions, none of which seem capable of embodying the will of the people. But the "essentials" have been safeguarded: The coast guards are paid by the European Union to stem the tide of migrants. From Syria to Ukraine, the spontaneous reaction of some revolutionaries and their supporters has been to regret the nonintervention of the "international community." Yet, when intervention did occur, it was simply another way of extinguishing or neutralizing the revolutionary "threat."

In Sudan, resistance committees displayed a healthy mistrust toward any foreign intervention in the revolutionary process. This did not prevent the military and militias from winning out. Foreign interference found another path, siding with the competing factions of the former regime, some supported by the United Arab Emirates, others by Egypt, drowning the popular revolution in a military war. The consequence has been massive displacement and appalling famine. The Sudanese revolution's tenacious nonalignment has earned it a number of determined enemies within and beyond its borders. Enemies prepared to "burn down the country" rather than risk revolutionary success.

No power whatsoever has ever really come to the aid of insurgent people. A few years ago, at an evening in support of the Syrian revolution somewhere in France, a member of the public asked, "But what can we do to help?" One of the activists present, a survivor of the siege of Homs, replied: "Send us anti-tank missiles!" Apart from the fact that the audience was not in a position to respond to such a request, it seemed to place any solidarity action with Syrian revolutionaries in the shadow of states. Was there no other way to help the revolution other than by calling on Western governments to intervene militarily against the regime, or deliver heavy weapons?

For us, this is not a moral question, even if for many dissidents in the centers it would be inconceivable to demonstrate to demand military intervention by NATO. Having access to weapons is a matter of survival for many insurgents, which even the most pacifist among us cannot fail to recognize. That comrades on the front lines of the Ukrainian, Libyan, or Palestinian resistance have called for military or tactical intervention by third powers to counter the ferocious repression unleashed against them is understandable. There's a whole debate to be had within revolutionary movements on the question of military intervention, the forms it can take, and its impact on the outcome of events: from no-fly zones to boots on the ground, from opening up new fronts to technical assistance and the provision of military equipment. We cannot move forward without a serious assessment of the balance of power on the ground. Nor may we revert to impotent purism in the hope of avoiding contradictions. But to be dependent on the military capabilities of certain states or armed factions and see this as the only practical way of contributing to the struggle is a sign of our resignation, an abandonment of the very possibility of revolution.

Empire will outlive the West

The world we live in is full of differences, pieces of a jigsaw puzzle that are distinct but compatible, forming an overall picture of where we live. Differences are not just about distance. They are not the result of backwardness: they cannot be overcome by "progress." In an era of monolithic beliefs, differences are denied, or crushed to suit a global system for managing resources, exchanges, and identities. A skillful interweaving of distinct but complementary systems of domination has turned us into subjects of an *empire* that is constantly being modulated and extended. Changes in alliances, in the balance of power, and of capital cities are on the surface. Although there were precapitalist empires that predated the nation-state and were non-Western, the expansion of capitalism unified Empire into a single whole. Thus Empire survived the official end of European colonial empires, became secularized, and succeeded in spreading a belief that no alternative is possible.

Empire is not merely the name of the world system in which we live, with its international institutions, global markets, unified language, and ideological framework, from which no corner of the world is excluded. It's also a particular way of perceiving the world as a vast board game where different allied or rival powers compete for wealth and spheres of influence. Empire is where states negotiate the most profitable division of labor and the "rules of engagement" that allow each player to hold its own in the game of mass murder in which they are engaged. Beyond the capitalist system, Empire refers to all the formal and informal institutions, codes, customs, and rules that govern the center's predation on the rest of the world. From Mexico City to Dubai, from Tokyo to Cape Town, from Beijing to Frankfurt, people in the centers of power talk, eat, dress, make agreements, and con each other in much the same way. Empire always finds its local relays. It adapts to all cultures, all religions, all styles of exercising power. It remains indifferent to intention, culture, and behavior, as long as its spokespeople continue to play the game.

The recent strengthening of bloc logic is less a struggle between different kinds of imperialism, and rather a struggle for imperial hegemony within the same world system. While the West may appear to be making a comeback these days, with its show of unity to cover up genocide in the name of "Israel's right to defend itself," this comeback does little to conceal a slow decline amply illustrated in the proletarianization of societies, galloping inflation, the rise of fascism, calamitous military interventions, the disorderly withdrawal of occupying troops, and the steady loss of commercial and diplomatic influence. On a different note, the apparent consensus in support of the Ukrainian resistance suggests a certain feverishness, with military aid provided in dribs and drabs that has never been equal to Russian aggression. The "decline of the West" would be good news if it meant the decline of Empire. But it's only its face that is changing. The conquering smiles on the faces of the BRICS (Brazil, Russia, India, China,

South Africa) leaders, who everywhere flaunt their opportunistic alliance, make clear that they are ready to take *their* place at the same game. As long as Empire exists, the struggle against it continues, always renewing its form and statements, which it will again try to swallow to get back on its feet.

"each generation must, in relative obscurity, face up to its mission: fulfill it or betray it"*

In the last century, an entire generation across the globe rose up and exposed itself to bullets, deportation, and torture, to drive European powers out of colonized territories. The revolutionary offensive of the colonized was a response to the domination exercised by white powers for more than a century. And, in the crucible of these struggles, in the maquis and prisons of the West, in the first liberated territories, the political consciences of those who would plan the future were forged. The forms and concepts available in this already globalized world were those of Western history: the nation-state, progress, planning, regional development, national identities, representative democracy, nationalism, socialism . . . Ousting colonialists was not enough: The same captivatingly modern master's tools were used to construct the postcolonial states, and they produced the same contradictions.

The promise opened up by the end of colonial

---

*   Frantz Fanon, *The Wretched of the Earth* (New York: Grove, 1963).

empires, in the wake of national revolutions, gave way to a colossal hangover. Flags, anthems, and currencies have changed. Domination continued in other forms. The national bourgeoisies and political elites that emerged from the independence movements often succumbed to authoritarianism. After sacrificing the most militant among them, the new political classes in the countries of the South took their share of the fruits of postcolonial exploitation. In Arab countries, for example, twenty-first-century uprisings shook the foundations of regimes that had remained unchanged or almost unchanged since the early days of colonization, most of which had become police states. Frozen in the historical postures of decolonization and frontline resistance to Western imperialism, the parties in power seemed able to stifle popular aspirations for change for all eternity. But the return of the people has reshuffled the deck. As the Algerian Hirak demonstrators proclaimed: The 2019 uprising attempted to finish the job of the unfinished revolution of 1962.

While a demand for democracy lies at the heart of many recent uprisings, it's hard to find a place where democracy is fully embodied. The "democratic ideal," as it's still presented in the West, can no longer conceal what a sham it is. One only needs to look at a few images from the American election in the spring of 2024 to be convinced—in one of the "greatest democracies in the world." Before Kamala Harris entered the race after the Democratic candidate's near-cerebral death, two white, rich, Christian men in their seventies were clinging to power, vying with each other in tackling their respective symptoms of senility, instead of having political debates about the future of the world—a world that the United States has largely dominated and shaped for more than seventy years. The "democratic" deadlock that this image signifies bears similarity to the fifth presidential candidacy of a mummified Bouteflika—whose final candidacy sparked off the 2019 revolt in Algeria.

Democracy is not a Western invention extending from the assemblies of Athens to the French Republic, and now being exported to Afghanistan and Iraq with bombs. From the Haudenesonee Confederacy in North America to the Haitian Revolution, via the fugitive territories of "Zomia" in Southeast Asia, throughout history countless peoples have developed egalitarian deliberative practices to organize communal life. Indeed, the hijacking of the concept of democracy by the West has made it repellent in some parts of the world. So how can we avoid abandoning the idea of *power to the people*? How can we combat the sham of liberal democracies without playing into the hands of authoritarian regimes?

stopping this world

The face of Empire is changing, the face of war is changing, and so our strategies and our objectives cannot remain the same. In addition to suffering under authoritarian or oligarchic regimes, we have to deal directly or indirectly with the consequences of competing imperialist offensives that can destroy the already precarious living conditions in our territories overnight. Hunger riots are a daily occurrence across the globe. Rival powers are taking turns to use "food as a weapon" in a world where societies' ability to be self-sufficient has been methodically destroyed and where the vagaries of the climate are making harvests more uncertain than ever. In 2024 Vladimir Putin has put the whole of the Mediterranean in his power by monopolizing wheat production on Ukraine's fertile plains, upon which most Mediterranean countries are dependent. Food sovereignty has thus become a central issue in any politics of emancipation, transforming ways of struggle on every continent. No revolutionary perspective today can ignore how to reappropriate the means to meet our basic needs.

In this new phase of open armed conflict, aggressive power strategies, and nationalist revival, we are faced with the contradiction between our desire for a cooperative world in which people can organize for subsistence, and the reality of permanent threats posed by interimperialist conflicts. Wouldn't a "liberated" area, or state, which voluntarily abandoned policies of accumulation and monopolization immediately be swallowed up by rival powers?

In many parts of the world, behind the façade of order imposed by the sovereign state, community or religious militias, mafias, territorial gangs, and transnational corporations exist, to whom the repression of our movements and control of our communities are delegated. So, invoking the end of the state as the only horizon for revolution is not enough. The idea seems completely alien to those of us who, living under failed states, are left at the mercy of gang leaders and war lords, with no recourse in the face of poverty, disease, famine, or natural disasters. Destroying or fragmenting the states that crush people will not be enough, nor will simply replacing those who embody them. It's only by coming together collectively and taking control of our basic needs for safety, health, access to housing, and food that we will be able to claim our independence from Empire beyond the moment of insurrection.

The world unified by Empire, whatever language it speaks, whatever god it prays to, whatever currency it uses—dollar, euro, yuan, or any other—is not compatible with any other. Its only outcome will be the extermination of life on earth. All it knows is hegemony: the world as one, counted, mapped, developed, and made uninhabitable by a macabre rush toward the end. If nothing is done, our end will come before theirs. There is no going back, just as there is no maintaining the status quo. There is only a forward march, sometimes resolute, sometimes hazardous, only knowing where we've come from. We must break out of our national prism and think of a policy that is internationalist from the outset—reconstructing a *world made up of a multitude of worlds*. Worlds that are compatible and in the process of becoming so, and that are themselves riven by struggles and contradictions. There's a need to build a common plan between these worlds. A plan that will enable us to circumvent Empire, hasten its fall, and imagine the aftermath.

revolution?

SOONER OR LATER, IT WILL FALL | RUPTURE BY INSISTENCE | THE ORGANIZATIONAL DILEMMA | CHOOSE BOLDNESS, MEASURE RISK | DEFENDING THE REVOLUTION | THE EVIDENCE OF POPULAR POWER

In 2011, what commentators called the "Arab Spring," insurgents called *thawra* (revolution). Revolution in Burkina Faso (2014), the "revolution of dignity" in Ukraine (2014), a "spring revolution" in Burma (Myanmar) (2021), the "revolution of our time" in Hong Kong (2019), Jina's revolution in Iran (2022). "Revolution! Revolution! Revolution!" chanted the crowd in yellow vests on the Champs-Élysée (2018), reminding the rich of Paris of a refrain that weighs like a threat they thought they'd gotten rid of for good.

A few years after its sensational comeback, the fact that so few are asking the revolutionary question is testimony to the strength of the counterrevolution underway. The fact that so many people have recognized themselves as revolutionaries is not a sign of misplaced enthusiasm or youthful reverie. We must never underestimate what the real movement is announcing, to do so risks being swept away by the torrents of history.

Revolution is not an event to be studied, a theory to be developed, a cold body to be dissected. It's a question asked of ourselves, the "we" that shapes this text. And contrary to what ideologues, intellectuals, and prophets have always asserted, the answer is never absolute or eternal; it can only be momentary, provisional, situational. A glimmer of truth. We have sought to gather the scattered fragments, assemble, and interrogate them to see what they might tell us about the future.

sooner or later, it will fall

Storming palaces and parliaments came back into fashion with the uprisings of 2011. For many participants, the revolution meant the fall of the regime. But the hopes raised by the fall of governments in Yemen, Libya, Egypt, Tunisia, and Ukraine were short-lived. Authoritarian or liberal takeovers, foreign intervention, economic crisis, civil war . . . Removing tyrants is not synonymous with the victory of revolution.

Conversely, the failure to topple regimes in Syria or Iran has not meant the absence of revolutionary achievement. The rejection of the compulsory hijab (veil) and control over "morality" imposed by the

Islamic Republic was a radical fracture. Likewise, Syrians' ability to organize themselves to administer territories liberated from the state collectively represented an irreversible break with Assad's totalitarianism. This explains why, thirteen years on, despite brutal counterinsurgency, the revolution's flag continues to fly high in the provinces of northern Syria that remain beyond regime control, as in the rebellious province of Sweida, in the south of the country. In both Syria and Iran, the revolution has proved an existential turning point and the regime's hold on bodies and minds has been partially broken. Sooner or later, they will fall.*

No single event can put an end to all forms of domination. For a long time, the *grand soir* was the image par excellence of revolution. But repeated failure to bring about profound and lasting change by "seizing central power," and the eternal appeals of traditional organizations to wait until "the conditions are right," have led many to abandon the ideal of the fall of the regime as a strategic horizon and look for other prospects for liberation. For many, since the end of the last century, revolution is a process that begins without waiting. A determined but gradual march toward profound transformation embodied in a constellation of events, acts, interventions, ideas, feelings,

---

* The last lines of this text were written at the beginning of September 2024. Three months later, the regime of Bashar al-Assad finally fell.

and everyday practices. "El tiempo de la revolución es ahora,"[*] say feminists in Argentina. Revolution is conceived as being no longer distant, but a way of life and a struggle *in the here and now.*

The challenge is to dismantle the structures that oppress us. The major strategic imperative is to stop sacrificing the means—or the struggle of some—in the name of an end that is always postponed. This conception of politics as *transformation*, rather than the conquest of power, relocates revolutionary politics in praxis and in the intimate, previously lacking in the work of so many organizations and activists. It's about building a radically new life, a new relationship to one's community, to desire, to money, to care, and even to one's struggle.

Viewing revolution as a process is not inconsistent with the conviction that the moment of insurrection is central to it. Whatever the outcome, an uprising is always a decisive event. Even in defeat, it leaves irrefutable and embodied experiences. Countless seeds grow in its wake. If, on the other hand, revolution does succeed in toppling a regime, then something promising and perilous is born.

rupture by insistence

To conceive of revolution without rupture, remaining oblivious to unexpected opportunities, would

---

[*] "The time for revolution is now."

risk allowing our actions to exist independently of the world around us. For many revolutionaries, revolution as a gradual process means building material and political autonomy, through collective or territorial forms of self-sufficiency. This quest to break away from dependence on the centers has spread to the forests, mountains, and cities of the world. The construction of autonomy has given rise to spaces that are firmly rooted in the world, and that run counter to the infernal march imposed by Empire. Autonomy can take many forms. It can be rooted in a thousand-year-old history, or be entirely new. It can be embodied in a local assembly, an agricultural cooperative, a community canteen, a neighborhood union, a transnational queer solidarity network, or a media collective.

Yet, the construction of autonomy, which is costly in terms of time and energy, can easily become avoidance if it ignores real historical changes and is not challenged by them. Ideologically "pure" insurrections can never exist. Moments of popular revolt are unique opportunities to multiply forces tenfold and scale up experiments. Otherwise, we run the risk of becoming an isolated, "alternative" niche, easily subsumed into capitalism or by the state. Remaining barricaded behind certainties and our own everyday experience condemns us to perpetual failure. The risk of conceiving autonomy as an unchanging form, punctuated by more or less agitation, locks us into cultural trench warfare, which we can only lose because of our adversaries' colossal resources. We cannot live as we want without dismantling apparatuses of power that regulate social life and control where we live. But we cannot dismantle apparatuses of power alone.

Uprisings break through isolation. They allow for giant leaps forward. They make for unprecedented coalitions and constitute a moment of mass offensive, without which there can be no tipping points or irreversible change. Whether we are members of an agricultural cooperative or a media collective, an affinity group or mass organization, being alert to the possibility of the real movement erupting enables us to deploy forces effectively in the brief moments of opportunity that may present themselves.

Process and event. Perhaps this is the thoroughgoing revolution, the intersection of two ways of seeing and experiencing revolution. On the one hand, the present, patient, ongoing construction of our autonomy, the meticulous preparation for our encounter, the strengthening of our forces. On the other, the eruptive and explosive nature of the uprising, with its exceptional concentration of energies, its unequaled deployment of popular power, its creativity. Thoroughgoing revolutions are made possible by sequences of uprisings that meet and exceed their limits, in search of that rupture through insistence, as a Chilean comrade said.

We never start from scratch. Every insurrection, every experiment in popular power, every assault on

Empire is part of a deeper movement, behind us and ahead of us at the same time, below the surface and looming over the horizon. A tidal wave starts out as an imperceptible current in the middle of the ocean. And it becomes one again after crashing against the shore. We need to learn to act as an undercurrent as much as a tsunami. Perhaps this is the full meaning of the mantra of Hong Kong's revolution: *Be water, my friend.*

the organizational dilemma

The popular mobilizations of our time have often been heterogenous and diffuse. They've rarely been led by traditional organizations, nor defined by pre-existing political ideologies. The more or less spontaneous and horizontal self-organization, impressive though it was in the early days, was insufficient. The decentralized nature of our movements was both their strength and their weakness. The lack of any consistent organizational capacity or medium- to long-term strategic vision, combined with the difficulty of maintaining street tactics, meant that we were caught between repression and co-optation. In some cases, we lacked organizations to take up the revolutionary cause.

In Ecuador during the 2019 revolt, major indigenous organizations and trade unions were able to mobilize millions of people from across the country and bring them to the capital to reinforce the ranks of insurgents. Due to their strength of appeal, logistical resources, and coordination skills, the movement was able to confront the authorities on several fronts and finally obtain the withdrawal of the contested government measures. This impressive capacity for mobilization reminds us of the potential strength of organizations, but we must also be mindful of their dangers.

Many have become disillusioned with historic organizations of the left because of their bureaucratic tendencies, their attempts to co-opt the movement, or their desire to direct it. Organizational intervention always carries the risk of limiting the spread of the uprising and curbing the radical nature of its demands, its creativity, and sometimes even its nascent popular institutions. Whether it comes from the far right, religious fundamentalists, or certain organized fringes on the left, there will always be groups seeking to push their own agenda during uprisings. Without organizational and strategic consistency, it's difficult to prevent these factions from seizing power, and we are left at the mercy of their strategies.

An organization is both a concentration of energy and resources and a network of connections capable of constituting a collective force. In certain contexts, organizations may be necessary, not only to prevent hijacking by reactionary or liberal forces but also to help a movement achieve its aims. But how can the power of organizations within an uprising be circumscribed? How can we guard against the centralizing effects that organizations inevitably produce? How can we build the strength of the movement as a whole and not just the strength of the organization? A genuinely revolutionary organization is at one with the movement, striving to nourish the strength of the emerging popular powers, keeping the flame of revolt alive at the risk of extinguishing itself. And it can only do this by avoiding imposing its own agenda, its own dogma, its own way of doing or saying things.

In many uprisings, behind the apparent spontaneity of forms of self-organization, we may detect connections built between groups that existed prior to the moment of insurrection: local communities, political affiliations, religious or traditional institutions, professional or sporting societies that together form a substratum that enables something other than chaos to be. But how can we, mid-turbulence, formulate a coherent strategy to coordinate a revolution? During the Sudanese revolution, the hybridization between the organizational experiences of the student movement, former Communist Party activists, and the forces born of the popular revolt allowed resistance committees to come into being. The most promising experiences have been those in which there has been an *encounter* between partisan forms, constructed over many years, and new forms born of the event. Encounters only happen when both parties are transformed. A willingness to change is essential for any revolutionary force. Make plans: but draw them in pencil.

choose boldness, measure risk

No single force can be expected to establish a plan for all. Thinking of ourselves as part of a movement that transcends us, rather than as an organization or chapel to be defended at all costs, means behaving and thinking in a complementary rather than competitive manner. Maximizing the power of a common movement means finding the best combination of tactics to suit the respective situations of each component part. The Kurdish movement combines armed struggle with the election of mayors and deputies to the Turkish assembly. Burma's pacifist resistance movement for democracy has transformed into an armed struggle with the support of a diaspora that raises funds through queer events and online video games. Lebanese revolutionaries have built self-managed cooperatives and have also tried to reclaim professional organizations.

Avoid fetishizing one mode of action over another and try out new hybridizations. Going against tactical and ideological rigidities opens up new ways of articulating strategies for transformation. No one can say a priori what a revolutionary act should be. A movement gains in strength if it listens to, explores, and connects the different spheres of struggle that challenge the status quo. It must avoid militant dogmatism and aesthetic posturing, without ever neglecting ethical development.

Ethical questions are not incidental to revolutionary strategy, they are at its heart. Working out *how* to do things together is essential. So is measuring the risks we're willing to take for ourselves and for others. Keep in touch with what mattered at the start. Always remember what sets us apart from counter-revolutionary forces. Such principles enable us to thread our way through the storm of an uprising. As our Argentinian comrades used to say, if we do not want to reproduce the kind of power we're fighting against, we must not confront it or regard it as a rival. As a result of the mirror effect, through facing and looking at each other, we always end up mimicking our opponents. When revolutionary forces hope to beat the centers at their own game, they become a deformed and misguided reflection of them.

The path of strategic articulation also involves learning from experience. In recent years, we have again seen how movements that focus on the institutional route, in a quest for concrete change at the expense of building political and material autonomy, are regularly co-opted. And those that assume they can pursue both insurrectionary and institutional avenues in parallel find themselves exhausted. In Argentina, feminists broke down the paralyzing dichotomy between reform and revolution by seeing potential victories in the implementation of direct institutional reforms, such as the legalization of abortion. But beset by fascist forces, after several defeats on the institutional terrain and unproductive alliances with a powerless and discredited progressivism, the movement found itself unable to preserve internal strength. The means for political autonomy was lost. There was no fallback strategy when the institutional route failed.

Both Syriza in Greece and Podemos in Spain seem to have reached the same impasse after they focused on institutional spaces of power: What followed was a disconnection with the popular mobilization, compromise with neoliberal policies, generalized disappointment, and a feeling of betrayal. But remaining outside institutions is neither an objective nor a question of principle. A reform, an election, and perhaps even a presidential candidacy can in certain situations serve the revolutionary cause. We must ensure that such moments serve to strengthen the revolutionary movement and its autonomy and are not merely a chance to launch the political career of inevitable opportunists. When it comes to tactics and devising strategies, inventiveness is what breaks new ground.

defending the revolution

When the centers lose political ground, weapons intervene. This grim fact condemns most revolutions to war. Resorting to armed struggle is rarely a strategic choice. It's the level of state violence that determines if and when revolutionaries are forced to pick up arms. Pacifism cannot defend itself against a state, or groups within it, that are prepared to exterminate an entire population to quell a revolt. But the arrival of arms in a revolutionary movement is always a threat to its survival because when they enter the scene, the whole movement is impacted. Many revolutionaries have said how militarization severed them from active participation in the insurrection, when "being a revolutionary" became synonymous with "carrying a gun." Women and gender dissidents in particular often find themselves marginalized by the militarization of an insurrection. The use of armed violence irreversibly marks the course of a movement and serves to legitimize ever more violent repression by the state against the population as a whole. Our primary concern should be that the taking up of weapons does not radically change a movement's objectives, composition, and political texture. When taking up arms is inevitable, efforts need to be made to prevent the armed struggle from becoming the sole horizon of the uprising. Survival on military terrain cannot be the sole lever.

When a state's armed forces defect, as in Tunisia and Egypt in 2011, something decisive is in play. Defectors often bring their weapons with them, but rarely enough to counter a state's arsenal. Access to weapons and the financial resources to buy them become the alpha and omega of revolutionary struggle, often justifying alliances that, however judicious they may seem at the time, prove dangerous, even fatal, before long.

Unfortunately, the military balance of power often determines scope for revolution. The profoundly asymmetrical nature of confrontation with the state apparatus and superpowers places revolutionaries at a significant disadvantage. Syria and Sudan, two of the most promising and thoroughgoing revolutions of our time, have had painful experience of this. Towns and villages were reduced to rubble and drowned in blood; millions were displaced from their homes. The trauma will take generations to heal.

Victory for a resistance or revolutionary movement often comes down not to having as many weapons as possible, but rather to preventing adversaries from using theirs. The question of defending the revolution is as much a military question as a political one. Whenever possible, the challenge may be to attempt, while there is still time, to deactivate the military apparatus as effectively as possible. Blockade barracks, imprison generals, disarm institutions. But even if successful, what then? What can be done when an outside intervention or an attempt at domestic containment tries to regain control by force? And even if that doesn't happen, what about the militias and armed gangs who, as in Haiti and Ecuador, try to take advantage of the situation? When weapons intervene, a popular uprising can easily turn into a cacophony of competing authoritarianisms, delivering people into the hands of warlords.

The relationship between the local and the transnational, and the nature of the links built between peoples, revolutionary forces, and popular organizations across the globe, are crucial to preventing revolts from becoming isolated. International support is a major asset on the revolutionaries' side, which can exert significant pressure depending on the situation. At best it can prevent bloodshed, and at least buy time to organize self-defense. This is one of the horizons of revolutionary internationalism.

the evidence of popular power

"Why build a 'counter-power'? We are the people. We should have power!" This reflection, formulated by a Yellow Vest protester at an assembly in France, is perhaps the best expression of the aspiration for popular power that we've heard. The revolution we seek is neither the refusal of power nor its negation. That would mean perpetually leaving power in the hands of our adversaries. We cannot be content to always be a dam, a break, an opposition, even permanent, to the domination of the centers. Popular power is, on the contrary, the active search and living construction of a collective way of forging a new legitimacy, of exercising a different kind of power.

Recent revolts everywhere have sought to increase popular power, or at least to prevent the confiscation of power by a few. Some, in Syria, Hong Kong, Ukraine, or Algeria, thought they were achieving this by demanding a democratic state; or by demanding the abolition or defunding of the police in the United States; or a permanent Citizens' Initiative Referendum in France; by ousting the French neocolonialists and their accomplices in West Africa; by establishing confederalism in Kurdistan or changing the constitution in Chile. The insurgents wanted more power, but that didn't always mean they wanted to govern.

Others, like some of us, thought that extending the power of the people meant above all building popular power in the heart and in the wake of revolt. Beginning to build from below, from what had already begun to mutate, the principles of self-government that could serve as the architecture for the aftermath of the uprising. Building autonomous power without leaving it to a few vanguards, leaders, officers, or new governments. Removing central power and building popular power.

After the fall of the regime, the resistance committees of the Sudanese revolution, faced with the contradictions and paralysis of the first transitional government, drew up a proposal for the future of the country, so as not to leave the field to the old guard politicians. The Charter for the Establishment of the People's Authority outlines a new form of governance. It proposes the establishment of a localized, bottom-up system of power in which the civil and popular forms of organization that emerged from the revolution retain a say in the legislative process and the balance of power. It also demands the fair distribution of the country's wealth and an end to plunder by foreign powers, whoever they may be. With this proposal, the Sudanese were trying to defend the revolution without resort to arms. Although the Sudanese revolution seems to have been cornered in a bloody impasse, it certainly has not said its last word. As a Sudanese comrade once said: "Revolution has become a religion in Sudan."

In Mexico, the struggle for the autonomy of popular powers and the *defense of the revolution* have never ceased since the first decade of revolts in 1910 that led to the establishment of the Mexican state. For over one hundred years, despite the Institutional Revolutionary Party's decades-long capture of power, the attempts at liberal counterrevolution supported by the United States, and the compromises of the social-democratic left, a patient strategic wisdom has been woven in every territory, from remote indigenous communities to the working-class districts of the big cities. Grassroots movements of slum dwellers or rural teachers' unions, indigenous councils, community police forces, neighborhood councils, and autonomous health facilities have flourished in a country that is known to be "one of the most violent in the world." Nowhere else has community power been taken so far. While these experiments are still threatened by many reactionary forces and face the authorities' corruption, they have demonstrated their ability to take root and resist for decades. *People Power* is the opposite of powerlessness. It means taking the time to climb the rungs of the ladder, one by one, and not relying on those who want to capture our votes. People Power. These two words in their naked simplicity. *Power* as the ability to act, to decide, to implement. *Popular* as diverse, as direct, as transversal, as here, as everywhere, and as now. Popular power as a guarantee against any further electoral betrayal, as an offensive against the status quo, as the only antidote to fascism.

If revolution is a question, then we can neither win nor lose. Only battles can be won or lost. Always partial, sometimes decisive, never definitive. Revolution is the inextinguishable yearning for *dignity*, and the constant search, for several millennia now, for *how* to embody it on this earth.

How can nascent popular powers be protected from the risk of civil war? Is there an alternative to taking up arms, or is it an inevitable horizon of revolution? Is the establishment of a revolutionary power on a "national" scale, in place of the one we are fighting, an indispensable stage in making change irreversible? Or, on the contrary, should we consolidate popular power everywhere to prevent it being brought to heel by the new state apparatus, however revolutionary? We do not have the answers to these questions, which so many revolutionaries have already asked. The search for a theory that would provide the secret formula for victory is a dead end. There is only experimentation, placing bets, and more or less fertile strategic compositions. Some will base their answers on the strength of revolutionary organizations, others on emerging forms of territorial power, still others on the unifying power of religions and ideologies. Others will base their responses on a clever mix of all of these.

The path of revolution is not a straight line. It will be like a streak of stars, a series of conflagrations lighting up the night, each one pointing the way more clearly than the last, until we finally pass the point of no return.

starting over

CREATING A TRANSNATIONAL SPACE FOR LIAISON | POOLING AND MULTIPLYING OUR RESOURCES | MAPPING A PLANET OF FRIENDLY PLACES | GIVING FLESH TO A TRANSNATIONAL REVOLUTIONARY CULTURE | BETWEEN THE IMPROBABLE AND THE IMPOSSIBLE

And at dawn, armed with ardent patience, we will enter the splendid cities

Over the last five years, following a number of gatherings, we've begun to weave a network that transcends borders, rooted in myriad spaces and territories intent on building popular powers. This is a network comprising individuals and collectives inspired by the cycle of popular uprisings that have taken place in the years since 2011; we see in these a source of energy and a signal of major upheavals to come.

We've opened up a space where the revolutionaries of Khartoum's resistance committees can exchange ideas and analysis with feminists and members of territorial assemblies in Santiago; where the determined youth of Sri Lanka's GotaGoGama villages mingle with participants in the ecological struggles of France and the United States; where grassroots movements from Mexico City's working-class neighborhoods talk to members of local councils from insurgent Syria, and Lebanese and Iraqi farmers connect with indigenous peoples of Abya Yala. Barely a month after the uprising in Iran in 2022, Iranian exiles were able to debate with activists from grassroots movements in West Africa what the fall of the regime meant and the meaning of the word "revolution."

From there, we set about laying the foundations for a new kind of transnational force. A force that could draw on the pooling of our experiences and analyses and give itself the means to ensure that they are followed up by action. A force capable of concretely supporting present and future movements and uprisings.

creating a transnational space for liaison

Our first task is to ensure that we are able to meet, to increase the number of connections between the various centers of the emerging revolutionary movement throughout the world. To create the material and logistical conditions for a planetary debate in which approaches to revolution are renewed. We want to create a space that will enable us to go beyond existing connections and enable the birth of a shared strategy. It is important that this new space should last, and be geographically diverse, in order that as many people as possible should recognize something of theirs in it, and something relevant to their experience and to their hopes.

pooling and multiplying our resources

There can be no revolutionary force without material power. Making our perspectives clear and explicit, broadening and multiplying movement between our territories offer us the possibility of finding material and financial resources, but also allies and tools which, once pooled, will increase our capacity to act.

We want to establish a network of material mutual aid as soon as possible, so that we can quickly offer support during wars, climatic disasters, or revolutions, and at the same time build the long-term infrastructures that will enable our struggles to become self-sustaining in the long term. The balance of these two timeframes is needed if our movements are to survive, maintain their independence, and grow in strength.

The resources available to us on our own small scale may rightly seem infinitesimal given the scale of the task. But we have all experienced circumstances where not only did everything seem possible but everything happened, with each gesture leading to dozens of others along the way. Revolutionary mutual aid, like courage, can make itself contagious when the time comes.

mapping a planet of friendly places

To meet and organize, we need places. Discreet but accessible places of welcome, to which anyone forced to flee their country of origin can turn. We need places of refuge, retreat, care, and protection, places where we can find a little respite and "recharge our batteries." Places dedicated to livelihood issues and training, but also places to dance, make music, share films, create together, and eat well. Many of these places already exist, but they are waiting to be placed on a common map. Connecting these places will be like a process of planetary neighborhooding, of *mujawara* as our Lebanese comrades say. It will materialize our common oath from one neighborhood to the next, from one village to the next, from one farm to the next.

Of course, we don't all have the same level of mobility. Building safe and dignified routes of exile, by imagining multiple interconnected territories and stages to facilitate escape and movement, is a major challenge—finding channels and tricks to enable us to bypass physical and administrative barriers and occasionally gather en masse in organized convoys. Let these routes also be stages for return journeys, coming and going, as state borders crack under the persistent action of our flows.

giving flesh to a transnational revolutionary culture

To disseminate our analyses, to compare them, to allow the experiences of our comrades from different parts of the world to be heard everywhere, so that together we can develop a political education worthy of our times. In the medium term, to put in place the means for a major cultural offensive in each of our countries to encourage the return of a nonaligned popular internationalism. Working on building synergies between different types of political, territorial, and community organizations; independent media; communication channels; and cultural venues.

The task before us is to restore legitimacy to the revolutionary perspective by preventing our struggles from facing isolation. Relating histories and experiences that our adversaries want to keep apart. Connecting different fronts within an international revolutionary movement both such as already exist and as are yet to be built. We can see the stars separated in the sky, or we can see them as constellations.

between the improbable and the possible

Every dream, every hope for a different life hangs in a fragile equilibrium and oscillates between the shadow of doubt and the glow of certainty. We stand at a crossroads where aspirations for change confront realities of a collapsing world. We can continue to watch as the Empire drags us into the abyss, affecting not to know; we can surrender to general panic or lie prostrate, awaiting the end; or we can meticulously organize an exit plan, betting we can extract a plausible future from an improbable present. We need to find a revolutionary horizon, not just in order to survive, but to live a life worth living.

Now is the time to build structures that can withstand the storms of tomorrow. Now is the time to extend and consolidate our connections. Our respective circumstances will continue to deteriorate, but tipping points of all kinds will create opportunities for change that we can turn to our advantage, provided we are ready. Every step we take, every obstacle we overcome, brings us a little closer to significant victories—victories that can offer some comfort to the souls of those we have lost in battle, who are waiting to rest in peace.

To structure this new force that we are calling for, to give shape to its action, there is still much to be done. Success will depend on responses to the proposal we are making in this text—on the number and determination of those willing to work with us.

We are aware of the magnitude of the task. We are learning from the failures of our elders. We know the many threats we face. The odds are not in our favor. Perhaps we will not turn the tide, become that tsunami.

But as a Catalan friend once said: "There are times when not to take risks is a risk not worth taking."